THROUGH THE YEAR WITH
POPE FRANCIS

DAILY REFLECTIONS

Through the Year with Pope Francis

Daily Reflections

Edited by Kevin Cotter

Our Sunday Visitor Publishing Division
Our Sunday Visitor
Huntington, Indiana 46750

Table of Contents

Acknowledgments

The quotations of Pope Francis are used with permission from the following sources:

- Homilies given at the Domus Sanctae Marthae, originally published by *L'Osservatore Romano*, copyright © 2013 by Libreria Editrice Vaticana.
- The Vatican website, www.vatican.va, copyright © 2013 by Libreria Editrice Vaticana.
- *Only Love Can Save Us: Letters, Homilies, and Talks of Cardinal Jorge Bergoglio* (Huntington, IN: Our Sunday Visitor, 2013).
- Jorge Mario Bergoglio and Abraham Skorka, *On Heaven and Earth: Pope Francis on Faith, Family, and the Church in the 21st Century* (Image, 2013).
- Antonio Spadaro, S.J., "A Big Heart Open to God," *America* magazine (September 30, 2013).

Unless otherwise noted, the Scripture citations used in this work are taken from the *Second Catholic Edition of the Revised Standard Version of the Bible* (RSV), copyright © 1965, 1966, and 2006 by the Division of Christian Education of the National Council of the Churches of Christ in the United States of America. Used by permission. All rights reserved.

Other Scripture citations are taken from the *Holy Bible, New International Version* (NIV), copyright © 1973, 1978, 1984 by International Bible Society. Used by permission of Zondervan Publishing House. All rights reserved.

Introduction

Pope Francis' election as the leader of the Catholic Church was shocking. An unexpected and almost unprecedented resignation by Pope Benedict XVI gave way to the election of our first Argentinian and Jesuit pope. Few had heard of and even fewer knew much about Cardinal Jorge Mario Bergoglio, but the reaction to his first few moments as Pope Francis were electric and caused a storm of media attention and commentary. This unanticipated beginning has been superseded by the actions and words of the pope during his papacy.

Pope Francis is a wonderful communicator. Like many great speakers, he does not always say something new, but rather something familiar in a way that gives new clarity and insight.

So, what is his message? Like popes before him, Pope Francis proclaims the message of Jesus, the message of the Gospel — a message that is, at times, alarming, comforting, unbelievable, simple, radical, and even somehow all of these things simultaneously. In his disarming and engaging way, Pope Francis allows us to hear this powerful message afresh once again.

This book of reflections will help you to explore this message in small portions suitable for prayer. Think of it as your daily protein shake or energy shot of the Gospel message, according to Pope Francis.

The material is set up so that you can not only read the words of Pope Francis but also reflect on their meaning for your life as you consider the questions that follow each meditation.

St. Francis de Sales, one of the great spiritual directors among the saints, offers six steps to prayer that can allow you to enter more deeply into meditation and conversation with the Lord:

1. **Place yourself in the presence of God.** Remember that God is near you. Take a moment to invite him into your time of prayer. Meet him as if you were meeting a friend.

2. **Ask God for his assistance.** Ask that he would help in your meditation. Pray that God uses this time to draw you closer to him.

3. **Read over a passage of Scripture or some other spiritual work.** In this case, your spiritual reading will be the words of Pope Francis, but also consider supplementing this with Scripture, the *Catechism of the Catholic Church*, or other spiritual readings.

4. **Take some time to reflect and think over what you have read.** Your goal is not necessarily to learn something but to enter more deeply into a relationship with Jesus and to understand yourself and God more intimately. Listen to what God is trying to tell you.

5. **Have a conversation with God about your reflections and thoughts.** In this step, you want to ask yourself: What stood out to you in your spiritual reading? What is God trying to tell you through what you just read? What feelings arise in your heart? Talk to God about these things.

6. **Conclude your time in prayer.** In your conclusion, St. Francis recommends thanking God for your time in prayer, making petitions for yourself and others, and developing a practical resolution. Take what insights you have gained and apply them to

your life in a practical way. For example, do you need to be more faithful to prayer? Do you need to forgive someone?

As St. Francis de Sales and many other spiritual writers make clear, there is no perfect method or process for prayer, which is ultimately the work of the Holy Spirit. The reflections I've provided following the pope's words are only meant to serve as prompts toward prayer; use them when you find them helpful, but don't be afraid to allow the Spirit to move you wherever he wishes.

May Pope Francis' words lead all of us to a deep relationship with God and a greater understanding of how to live his mission in our lives.

With hope in the Divine Will,

KEVIN COTTER
October 1, 2013
Feast of St. Thérèse of the Child Jesus

The Gaze of the Lord

I ask you: How do you abide in the presence of the Lord? When you visit the Lord, when you look at the tabernacle, what do you do? Without speaking ... "But I speak, I talk, I think, I meditate, I listen ..." Very good! But do you let yourself be looked at by the Lord? Letting ourselves be gazed upon by the Lord. He looks at us and this is itself a way of praying. Do you [let] yourselves be gazed upon by the Lord? But how do you do this? You look at the tabernacle and you let yourselves be looked at ... it is simple! "It is a bit boring, I fall asleep." Fall asleep then, sleep! He is still looking at you. But know for sure that he is looking at you!

— Address, September 27, 2013

Reflection: Spend some time in the Lord's gaze. How does he view you? What does he think about your life?

Open Yourself to Him

Christ's love and his friendship are not an illusion — Jesus on the Cross shows how real they are — nor are they the privilege of a few.

You will discover this friendship and feel its full fruitfulness and beauty if you seek it with sincerity, open yourselves to him with trust, cultivate your spiritual life with perseverance, receiving the sacraments, meditating on Sacred Scripture, praying assiduously, and living with deep involvement in the Christian community.

— Message, June 21, 2013

Reflection: What's one practical thing you can do to strengthen your relationship with Jesus this week? Use Pope Francis' examples as a starting point.

The Powerful Name of Jesus

FEAST OF THE MOST HOLY NAME OF JESUS

In a homily at the Domus Sanctae Marthae, Pope Francis spoke of an employee, the father of eight children, who had worked in the bishop's office in Buenos Aires for thirty years.

Before going out, before going to do any of the things he had to do, he would whisper to himself: "Jesus!" I once asked him, "Why do you keep saying Jesus?" "When I say 'Jesus,' " this humble man answered me, "I feel strong, I feel able to work because I know he is beside me, that he is preserving me." [This man] had not studied theology. He had only the grace of Baptism and the power of the Spirit. His witness did so much good for me. The name of Jesus. There is no other name.

— Homily, Domus Sanctae Marthae, April 5, 2013

Reflection: According to the Letter to the Hebrews, Jesus forever lives to intercede for us (7:25). Call on Jesus' name when you need his help.

Prayer of the Heart

I ask you all ... but reply in the silence of your heart, not aloud: Do I pray? Do I speak with Jesus, or am I frightened of silence? Do I allow the Holy Spirit to speak in my heart? Do I ask Jesus: What do you want me to do, what do you want from my life? This is training. Ask Jesus, speak to Jesus, and if you make a mistake in your life, if you should fall, if you should do something wrong, don't be afraid. Jesus, look at what I have done, what must I now do? Speak continually with Jesus, in the good times and in the bad, when you do right and when you do wrong. Do not fear him! This is prayer.

— Address, World Youth Day, July 27, 2013

Reflection: What scares you about prayer? Silence? Your sins? In your heart, talk to Jesus as a friend about what is going on in your life.

Image of God

What is the image we have of God? Perhaps he appears to us as a severe judge, as someone who curtails our freedom and the way we live our lives. But the Scriptures everywhere tell us that God is the Living One, the one who bestows life and points the way to fullness of life.

— Homily, June 16, 2013

Reflection: What is your image of God? Is he a God who is alive and who cares for you? Trust that he is leading you to the fullness of life.

The Fear of God's Newness

Newness always makes us a bit fearful, because we feel more secure if we have everything under control, if we are the ones who build, program, and plan our lives in accordance with our own ideas, our own comfort, our own preferences.... The newness which God brings into our life is something that actually brings fulfillment, that gives true joy, true serenity, because God loves us and desires only our good.

— Homily, Mass With the Ecclesial Movements
on Pentecost, May 19, 2013

Reflection: Who is in control of your life — you or God? How can you invite the newness of God into your life right now?

The Merciful Father

God always thinks with mercy: do not forget this. God always thinks mercifully. He is the merciful Father! God thinks like the father waiting for the son and goes to meet him, he spots him coming when he is still far off.... What does this mean? That he went every day to see if his son was coming home: this is our merciful Father. It indicates that he was waiting for him with longing on the terrace of his house.

— General Audience, March 27, 2013

Reflection: If God is like the merciful father in the parable of the prodigal son (see Luke 15:11-32), what is God waiting for you to do in your life right now?

Tidy Christians

One of the characteristics of those stuffy, neat and tidy Christians — of those hypocrites and those whitewashed tombs — is that they are always criticizing others, always speaking ill of others, whether family members, neighbors, or coworkers. In the back of their minds, they are simply repeating what that Pharisee said as he stood in front of the altar: "I thank God I am not like this or like that." They are repeating the words of a famous tango that says, "Shame on you, neighbor, for wearing white after you have sinned." Yet they themselves are criticizing.

That is the first characteristic of a stuffy, neat and tidy Christian, of a hypocrite, of a Pharisee: always feeling the need to criticize others.

— *Only Love Can Save Us*, Homily, September 24, 2011

Reflection: What causes you to criticize others? How can you give this struggle over to Jesus?

Part-Time Christians

We are not Christian "part-time," only at certain moments, in certain circumstances, in certain decisions; no one can be Christian in this way — we are Christian all the time! Totally!

— General Audience, May 15, 2013

Reflection: When do you find it hard to be a Christian? What is God calling you to do about these situations?

A Culture of Encounter

When leaders in various fields ask me for advice, my response is always the same: dialogue, dialogue, dialogue. The only way for individuals, families, and societies to grow, the only way for the life of peoples to progress, is via the culture of encounter, a culture in which all have something good to give and all can receive something good in return.

Others always have something to give me, if we know how to approach them in a spirit of openness and without prejudice.... Today, either we take the risk of dialogue, we risk the culture of encounter, or we all fall; this is the path that will bear fruit.

— Address, July 27, 2013

Reflection: What can you do specifically to encourage a culture of encounter and dialogue with the people you interact with every day? What conversations do you need to have?

Bigger Than the World Cup!

Jesus offers us something bigger than the World Cup! Something bigger than the World Cup! Jesus offers us the possibility of a fruitful life, a life of happiness; he also offers us a future with him, an endless future, in eternal life. That is what Jesus offers us. But he asks us to pay admission, and the cost of admission is that we train ourselves "to get in shape," so that we can face every situation in life undaunted, bearing witness to our faith.

— Address, World Youth Day, July 27, 2013

Reflection: What's your "World Cup"? What competes with Jesus in your life? Where do you need to "get in shape"?

Pope Francis' Father

My father went to Argentina as a young man full of illusions "of making it in America." And he suffered in the dreadful recession of the 1930s. They lost everything! There was no work! And in my childhood I heard talk of this period at home.... I never saw it, I had not yet been born, but I heard about this suffering at home, I heard talk of it. I know it well! However, I must say to you: "Courage!" Nevertheless, I am also aware that for my own part I must do everything to ensure that this term "courage" is not a beautiful word spoken in passing! May it not be merely the smile of a courteous employee, a Church employee who comes and says "Be brave!" No! I don't want this!

I want courage to come from within me and to impel me to do everything as a pastor, as a man. We must all face this challenge with solidarity, among you — also among us — we must all face with solidarity and intelligence this historic struggle.

— Address, Meeting With Workers, September 22, 2013

Reflection: What gives you courage? How do you find courage when you are afraid or worried? Only in the Lord can we find true courage. Ask him for it, and help others to find it.

Draw Near to God

I would also like to say to anyone who feels far away from God and the Church, to anyone who is timid or indifferent, to those who think they can no longer change: The Lord calls you, too, to become part of his people, and he does this with great respect and love! He invites us to be part of this people, the People of God!

— General Audience, June 12, 2013

Reflection: In the Letter of James we read, "Draw near to God and he will draw near to you" (4:8). Ask God for the wisdom to take steps toward him.

A Gift From God

In the Gospel, Jesus tells Nicodemus that he needs to be born from on high, from water and from the Spirit in order to enter the Kingdom of God (cf. John 3:3-5). It is through Baptism that we are introduced into this people, through faith in Christ, a gift from God that must be nourished and cultivated throughout our life.

— General Audience, June 12, 2013

Reflection: In Baptism, and in all of the sacraments of the Church, the Lord gives us an abundant amount of grace, but we must receive and use this grace. How can you cultivate God's gift to you? Can you take time to pray after Mass? Can you invite someone to Mass?

Stealing From the Poor

Let us remember well, however, that whenever food is thrown out it is as if it were stolen from the table of the poor, from the hungry! I ask everyone to reflect on the problem of the loss and waste of food, to identify ways and approaches which, by seriously dealing with this problem, convey solidarity and sharing with the underprivileged.

— General Audience, June 5, 2013

Reflection: In America, we waste over 40 percent of our food. How might you use food in a way that both respects this gift of God and also frees up some of your resources to help feed the poor?

What Does It Mean to Be a Spiritual Being?

When we say that a Christian is a spiritual being, we mean just this: The Christian is a person who thinks and acts in accordance with God, in accordance with the Holy Spirit. But I ask myself: And do we, do we think in accordance with God? Do we act in accordance with God? Or do we let ourselves be guided by the many other things that certainly do not come from God?

Each one of us needs to respond to this in the depths of his or her own heart.

— General Audience, May 8, 2013

Reflection: In what areas of your life do you think with the mind of the world rather than in accordance with God?

The Sins of the Faithful

Still today some say: "Christ yes, the Church no." Like those who say "I believe in God but not in priests." ... In those who make up the Church, pastors and faithful, there are shortcomings, imperfections, and sins. The Pope has these too — and many of them; but what is beautiful is that when we realize we are sinners we encounter the mercy of God, who always forgives.

Never forget it: God always pardons and receives us into his love of forgiveness and mercy.

— General Audience, May 29, 2013

Reflection: Whom is God asking you to forgive? Someone in the Church? Your family? Yourself?

Manifested in Love

Love shares everything it has and reveals itself in communication. There is no true faith that is not manifested in love. And love is not Christian love if it is not generous and concrete. A decidedly generous love is a sign of faith and an invitation to faith.

— *Only Love Can Save Us*, Lenten Letter, February 22, 2012

Reflection: Choose one concrete and generous way to love someone today.

I Am a Sinner

Jesus doesn't want us to follow a path of self-sufficiency. In order to be good Christians, we need to recognize that we are sinners. If we don't recognize we're sinners, we're not good Christians. This is the first condition. But we must be specific: "I am a sinner because of this, because of that...." This is the first condition for following Jesus.

— *Only Love Can Save Us*, Homily, September 24, 2011

Reflection: Think about your thoughts, words, and actions this last week. When have you sinned?

With Truth and Sincerity

Letting Christ make us his own always means straining forward to what lies ahead, to the goal of Christ (cf. Philippians 3:14), and it also means asking oneself with truth and sincerity: What have I done for Christ? What am I doing for Christ? What must I do for Christ?

— Homily, July 31, 2013

Reflection: In the silence of your heart, think about the questions that Pope Francis has asked.

Daily Martyrdom

FEAST OF ST. AGNES

But what does it mean "to lose one's life for the sake of Jesus"? This can happen in two ways: explicitly by confessing the faith, or implicitly by defending the truth. Martyrs are the greatest example of losing one's life for Christ.... However, there is also daily martyrdom, which may not entail death but is still a "loss of life" for Christ, by doing one's duty with love, according to the logic of Jesus, the logic of gift, of sacrifice.

— Angelus address, June 23, 2013

Reflection: How can the logic of Jesus change the way you see your life? What daily martyrdom is God asking you to offer up to him?

Pray for the Unborn

In a frail human being, each one of us is invited to recognize the face of the Lord, who in his human flesh experienced the indifference and solitude to which we so often condemn the poorest of the poor, whether in developing countries or in wealthy societies. Every child who, rather than being born, is condemned unjustly to being aborted, bears the face of Jesus Christ, bears the face of the Lord, who even before he was born, and then just after birth, experienced the world's rejection.

— Address, September 20, 2013.

Reflection: Today marks the anniversary of *Roe v. Wade*, which legalized abortion in the United States. Pray and fast for the end of abortion in the world.

Seeking Us

God created us so that we might live in a profound relationship of friendship with him, and even when sin broke off this relationship with him, with others, and with creation, God did not abandon us. The entire history of salvation is the story of God, who seeks out human beings, offers them his love, and welcomes them.

— General Audience, May 29, 2013

Reflection: Jesus wants a profound relationship with you. Have you entered into a relationship with Jesus before? Commit or re-commit your life to him.

Like Mary

FEAST OF OUR LADY OF PEACE

Mary is the woman who welcomes and accompanies life to the end, amid all life's difficulties and all life's joys. Mary is the woman who, in a day like today, welcomes life and accompanies it to its fullness. But her work is not over yet because she continues to accompany us in the life of the Church so that it may go forward. She is a woman of silence, of patience, who bears pain, faces difficulties, and yet knows how to rejoice deeply in the joy of her Son.

— *Only Love Can Save Us*, Homily,
Feast of the Annunciation, March 25, 2011

Reflection: Like Mary, how can you face the difficulties of this world while still having joy? What difficulty do you face now?

One Weapon

FEAST OF THE CONVERSION OF ST. PAUL

St. Paul has but one weapon: the message of Christ and the gift of his entire life for Christ and for others. It is precisely this readiness to lay himself open, personally, to be consumed for the sake of the Gospel, to make himself all things to all people, unstintingly, that gives him credibility and builds up the Church.

— Homily, June 29, 2013

Reflection: Would people know that you are a Christian by your daily example? In what one area can you grow so that your daily life witnesses to your faith?

Poor and for the Poor

Francis of Assisi. For me, he is the man of poverty, the man of peace, the man who loves and protects creation; these days we do not have a very good relationship with creation, do we? He is the man who gives us this spirit of peace, the poor man.... How I would like a Church which is poor and for the poor!

— Address, March 16, 2013

Reflection: St. Francis of Assisi became a saint in stages, not all at once. Ask him to pray for you so that you grow in love for the poor and for the Church as the Church of the poor.

Our Conscience

This is why we must learn to listen to our conscience more. But be careful! This does not mean following my own ego, doing what interests me, what suits me, what I like.... It is not this!

The conscience is the interior place for listening to the truth, to goodness, for listening to God; it is the inner place of my relationship with him, the One who speaks to my heart and helps me to discern, to understand the way I must take and, once the decision is made, to go forward, to stay faithful.

— Angelus address, June 30, 2013

Reflection: When you have questions that hinge on matters of conscience, do you find the books and mentors who can help you to think according to the mind of the Church? Ask God for the grace to do this, regardless of the consequences.

He Is With You

Some people might think: "I have no particular preparation, how can I go and proclaim the Gospel?" My dear friend, your fear is not so very different from that of Jeremiah, as we have just heard in the reading, when he was called by God to be a prophet. "Ah, Lord God! Behold, I do not know how to speak, for I am only a youth."

God says the same thing to you as he said to Jeremiah: "Be not afraid … for I am with you to deliver you" (Jeremiah 1:6, 8). He is with us!
— Homily, World Youth Day, Closing Mass, July 28, 2013

Reflection: What do you fear when you think about proclaiming the Gospel? Ask God to be with you and find someone to help equip you for the task.

Dream of Great Things!

Have you thought about the talents that God has given you? Have you thought of how you can put them at the service of others? Do not bury your talents! Set your stakes on great ideals, the ideals that enlarge the heart, the ideals of service that make your talents fruitful.

Life is not given to us to be jealously guarded for ourselves, but is given to us so that we may give it in turn. Dear young people, have a deep spirit! Do not be afraid to dream of great things!

— General Audience, April 24, 2013

Reflection: What talents has God given you? Tell God about your dreams of using them for others and for him.

A Great "Yes!"

The commandments are not a litany of prohibitions — you must not do this, you must not do that, you must not do the other; on the contrary, they are a great "Yes!": a yes to God, to Love, to life.

— Homily, June 16, 2013

Reflection: It's easy to see God as a rule-giver and to fear his punishments. But, when we see him as a loving father, it can completely change our perspective. Where is God asking you to follow him out of love and not fear?

Crossing the Deserts of Life

Man of every time and place desires a full and beautiful life, just and good, a life that is not threatened by death, but can still mature and grow to fullness. Man is like a traveler who, crossing the deserts of life, thirsts for the living water: gushing and fresh, capable of quenching his deep desire for light, love, beauty, and peace.

We all feel this desire! And Jesus gives us this living water: he is the Holy Spirit, who proceeds from the Father and whom Jesus pours out into our hearts. "I came that they may have life, and have it abundantly," Jesus tells us (John 10:10).

— General Audience, May 8, 2013

Reflection: What desires are on your heart today? Ask God to fulfill them in his way.

A Place of Mercy

May the Church be a place of God's mercy and hope, where all feel welcomed, loved, forgiven, and encouraged to live according to the good life of the Gospel. And to make others feel welcomed, loved, forgiven, and encouraged, the Church must be with doors wide open so that all may enter. And we must go out through these doors and proclaim the Gospel.

— General Audience, June 12, 2013

Reflection: How can you make the Church a more welcoming, merciful place? Who is Jesus calling you to reach out to? Find someone this week to encourage.

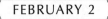

Obey

FEAST OF THE PRESENTATION OF THE LORD

What does obeying God mean? Does it mean that we must behave like slaves? No, whoever obeys God is free; he is not a slave! And how can this be? It seems like a contradiction.... The word "obey" comes from Latin, and means to listen, to hear others. Obeying God is listening to God, having an open heart to follow the path that God points out to us.

Obedience to God is listening to God, and it sets us free.

— Homily, Domus Sanctae Marthae, April 11, 2013

Reflection: Take some time to listen to God. What path is he asking you to follow?

Simple but Important

It is urgently necessary to find new forms and new ways to ensure that God's grace may touch the heart of every man and of every woman and lead them to him. We are all simple but important instruments of his; we have not received the gift of faith to keep it hidden, but, rather, to spread it so that it can illumine a great many of our brethren on their journey.

— Address, May 17, 2013

Reflection: Ask God to help you realize your ability to be his important instrument. You have gifts and talents no one else has. You have relationships and connections that others do not. Pray for the opportunities and courage to share your faith.

It Cannot Be So!

Nevertheless, men and women are sacrificed to the idols of profit and consumption: it is the "culture of waste." ... If there are children in so many parts of the world who have nothing to eat, that is not news; it seems normal. It cannot be so!

And yet these things enter into normality: that some homeless people should freeze to death on the street — this doesn't make news. On the contrary, when the stock market drops ten points in some cities, it constitutes a tragedy.... In this way, people are thrown aside as if they were trash.

— General Audience, June 5, 2013

Reflection: Jesus calls us to think differently about the poor (see Matthew 25:31-46). Are you doing any of the works of mercy that he asks of us? If not, why not?

What Jesus Wants

Jesus wants to be your friend, your brother, a teacher of truth and life who reveals to you the route to follow in order to reach happiness, the fulfillment of yourselves in accordance with God's plan for each one of you. And Jesus' friendship, which brings us the mercy and love of God, is "free," a pure gift. He asks nothing of you in exchange; he only asks you to welcome him.

Jesus wants to love you for what you are, even in your frailty and weakness, so that moved by his love, you may be renewed.

— Message, June 21, 2013

Reflection: Think about an area of weakness in your life. How can you allow the Lord to renew you in this area?

Close to Each One of Us

Dear friends, the experience of WYD [World Youth Day] reminds us of history's truly great piece of news: the Good News. Even if it is not splashed across the newspapers and does not appear on television, we are loved by God who is our Father and who sent his Son, Jesus, to make himself close to each one of us and to save us.

He sent Jesus to save us, to forgive all of us, for he always forgives: he always pardons because he is good and merciful.

— General Audience, September 4, 2013

Reflection: Reflect on God's love for you. He wants to be close to you. How can you draw near to him?

Not Like a Fairy With a Magic Wand

Time is the messenger of God: God saves us in time, not in a moment. At times, he works miracles, but in everyday life he saves us through time.

Sometimes we think that if the Lord comes into our life, he will change us. Yes, we do change: it is called conversion. But he does not act like "a fairy with a magic wand." No. He gives you the grace and he says, as he said to everyone he healed: "Go, walk."

— Homily, Domus Sanctae Marthae, April 12, 2013

Reflection: Where does your life still need to change? What steps toward conversion can you take this week?

Step Forward

If up till now you have kept him at a distance, step forward. He will receive you with open arms. If you have been indifferent, take a risk: you won't be disappointed.

If following him seems difficult, don't be afraid, trust him, be confident that he is close to you, he is with you and he will give you the peace you are looking for and the strength to live as he would have you do.

— Homily, Easter Vigil, March 30, 2013

Reflection: What makes you afraid of following Jesus? Ask him to help you get at the root of your fear and to surrender it to him.

The Grace We Need

In our personal life, in our private lives ... the Spirit pushes us to take a more evangelical path, and we [say]: "But no, it goes like this, Lord." ... Do not put up resistance to the Holy Spirit: this is the grace for which I wish we would all ask the Lord; docility to the Holy Spirit, to that Spirit who comes to us and makes us go forward on the path of holiness.

— Homily, Domus Sanctae Marthae, April 16, 2013

Reflection: Today, try to invite the Holy Spirit into your life throughout the day. Ask God for the ability to be docile.

Take Courage

May [the Holy Spirit] give to all of us apostolic fervor; may he also give us the grace to feel uncomfortable about certain aspects of the Church which are too relaxed; the grace to go forward to the existential outskirts. The Church is in great need of this! Not only in faraway lands, in young churches, to peoples who do not yet know Jesus Christ. But here in the city, right in the city, we need Jesus Christ's message.

We thus ask the Holy Spirit for this grace of apostolic zeal: be Christians with apostolic zeal. And if we make others uncomfortable, blessed be the Lord. Let's go, and as the Lord says to Paul: "Take courage!"

— Homily, Domus Sanctae Marthae, May 16, 2013

Reflection: What makes you uncomfortable about the Church today? Ask the Holy Spirit for wisdom to understand the teaching and mission of the Church and for zeal to bring others into the Body of Christ.

Mary Our Mother

FEAST OF OUR LADY OF LOURDES

Mary saw many difficult moments in her life, from the birth of Jesus, when "there was no place for them in the inn" (Luke 2:7), to Calvary (cf. John 19:25). And like a good mother, she is close to us, so that we may never lose courage before the adversities of life, before our weakness, before our sins: she gives us strength, she shows us the path of her Son.

— Address, May 4, 2013

Reflection: Have you ever experienced Mary's ability to bring you close to Jesus? Think about her life and the challenges she endured. Look to her to give you strength to face your challenges this week.

Service, Humility, Love

Benedict XVI, with great wisdom, often reminded the Church that although man frequently equates authority with control, dominion, success, for God authority is always synonymous with service, humility, love; it means entering the logic of Jesus, who kneels to wash the apostles' feet.

— Address, May 8, 2013

Reflection: Where do you seek control? How can you replace these desires with service?

Go on the Offensive

Be active members! Go on the offensive! Play down the field, build a better world, a world of brothers and sisters, a world of justice, of love, of peace, of fraternity, of solidarity. Play always on the offensive!

— Address, World Youth Day, Prayer Vigil, July 27, 2013

Reflection: What can you do this week to "go on the offensive" in order to make our world a better place?

A Difficult Science

The Lord loves us tenderly. The Lord knows the beautiful science of caresses — God's tenderness. He does not love us with words. He approaches us, and in being close to us gives us his love with the deepest possible tenderness.

More difficult than loving God is letting ourselves be loved by him. "Lord, I want to love you but teach me the difficult science, the difficult habit of letting myself be loved by you."

— Homily, Domus Sanctae Marthae, June 7, 2013

Reflection: Why is it so hard to let ourselves be loved by God? How can we get better at this difficult science?

God Accompanies Us

Ask yourselves: "How much space do I give to the Lord? Do I stop to talk with him?" Ever since we were children, our parents have taught us to start and end the day with a prayer, to teach us to feel that the friendship and the love of God accompanies us. Let us remember the Lord more in our daily life!

— General Audience, May 1, 2013

Reflection: Try to recall the presence of God in your life throughout the day, and say a short prayer when you do. See if you are able to do this at least three times today.

Lifeless Church

When the Church loses ... apostolic courage, she becomes a lifeless Church. Orderly, perhaps — nice, very nice — but barren, because she has lost the courage to go to the outskirts, where there are so many people who are victims of idolatry, worldliness, and weak thought....

Those who do not walk for fear of making a mistake make the most serious mistake.

— Homily, Domus Sanctae Marthae, May 8, 2013

Reflection: How is God calling you to be courageous in your everyday life? Who does he want you to reach out to?

Legalists

Jesus [says]: "Truly I say to you, the tax collectors and the harlots go into the kingdom of God before you" (Matthew 21:31). Jesus puts things in their proper place. He tells us that our Father in heaven is not a father who makes a pact with legalists. He is a Father of mercy.

— *Only Love Can Save Us*, Homily, September 24, 2011

Reflection: Legalists obey rules for the sake of rules. Children of God follow rules because of their relationship with the Father of mercy. How can you more deeply rely on God's mercy?

Spirit of Unity

The Holy Spirit would appear to create disorder in the Church, since he brings the diversity of charisms and gifts; yet all this, by his working, is a great source of wealth, for the Holy Spirit is the Spirit of unity, which does not mean uniformity, but which leads everything back to harmony.

— Homily, Mass With the Ecclesial Movements on Pentecost, May 19, 2013

Reflection: How is the Holy Spirit developing harmony in your parish? How can you support his movement? Where is he calling you to use your charisms and gifts?

Miracles Happen

Miracles happen. But prayer is needed! Prayer that is courageous, struggling, and persevering, not prayer that is a mere formality.

— Twitter, May 24, 2013

Reflection: What intention do you have on your heart? Pray for it each day and throughout the day.

Real Power Is Love

Pursuing and accumulating power as some form of adrenaline ... leads to self-destruction.... Real power is love; love that empowers others, love that sparks initiatives, love that no chain can hold because this love is capable of loving even on the cross or on a deathbed. It has no need of youthful beauty, recognition or approval, money or prestige. It simply flows forth and is unstoppable. When slandered or defeated, it unquestionably acquires greater recognition.

The Jesus who was weak and insignificant in the eyes of politicians and the powerful of the land revolutionized the world.

— *Only Love Can Save Us*, Homily, May 25, 2012

Reflection: Make a sincere act of love today. Be a revolutionary.

Evangelization Is Done on Your Knees

Listen well: "Evangelization is done on one's knees." Without a constant relationship with God, the mission becomes a job.... No. It is not a job, but rather something else. The risk of activism, of relying too much on structures, is an ever-present danger. If we look toward Jesus, we see that prior to any important decision or event he recollected himself in intense and prolonged prayer.

Let us cultivate the contemplative dimension, even amid the whirlwind of more urgent and heavy duties. And the more the mission calls you to go out to the margins of existence, let your heart be the more closely united to Christ's heart, full of mercy and love. Herein lies the secret of pastoral fruitfulness, of the fruitfulness of a disciple of the Lord!

— Homily, Mass With Seminarians and Novices, July 7, 2013

Reflection: Consider one step you can take to deepen your faithfulness to prayer despite your busyness. Can you make that step a priority until it becomes a habit?

Don't Be Afraid of Your Weakness

FEAST OF THE CHAIR OF ST. PETER

Let us also remember Peter: three times he denied Jesus, precisely when he should have been closest to him; and when he hits bottom, he meets the gaze of Jesus, who patiently, wordlessly, says to him: "Peter, don't be afraid of your weakness; trust in me." Peter understands, he feels the loving gaze of Jesus, and he weeps.

How beautiful is this gaze of Jesus — how much tenderness is there! Brothers and sisters, let us never lose trust in the patience and mercy of God!

— Homily, Divine Mercy Sunday, April 7, 2013

Reflection: When you sin today, quickly turn to the loving gaze of Jesus.

The Power to Renew

Jesus does not force you to be a Christian. But if you say you are a Christian, you must believe that Jesus has all power — and is the only one who has the power — to renew the world, to renew your life, to renew your family, to renew the community, to renew all things.

— *Only Love Can Save Us*, Homily, February 18, 2012

Reflection: What area of your life needs to be renewed? How can you trust in Jesus' power for this renewal?

The Dynamic of Hope

Anyone exercising a role of leadership — allow me to say, anyone whom life has anointed as a leader — needs to have practical goals and to seek specific means to attain them. At the same time, there is always the risk of disappointment, resentment, and indifference if our plans and goals do not materialize.

Here I would appeal to the dynamic of hope that inspires us to keep pressing on, to employ all our energies and abilities on behalf of those for whom we work, accepting results, making it possible to strike out on new paths, being generous even without apparent results, yet keeping hope alive, with the constancy and courage that comes from accepting a vocation as leader and guide.

— Address, July 27, 2013

Reflection: What role does hope play in your life? Do you allow yourself to hope? Ask the Lord to help you cultivate this critical virtue.

Economic Humanism

In many places, generally speaking, due to the economic humanism that has been imposed in the world, the culture of exclusion, of rejection, is spreading. There is no place for the elderly or for the unwanted child; there is no time for that poor person in the street. At times, it seems that for some people, human relations are regulated by two modern "dogmas": efficiency and pragmatism.... [H]ave the courage to go against the tide of this culture. Be courageous!

— Homily, World Youth Day, July 27, 2013

Reflection: In your life, where do you see the culture of efficiency and pragmatism at work? How can you courageously reject this culture?

Are You Brave Enough?

You, are you brave enough for this, do you have the courage to hear the voice of Jesus? It is beautiful to be missionaries! ... Everyone must be a missionary, everyone can hear that call of Jesus and go forth and proclaim the Kingdom!

— Angelus address, July 7, 2013

Reflection: What keeps you from hearing Jesus' call? Ask him how he wants *you* to proclaim his kingdom.

People Are Waiting for the Gospel

We cannot keep ourselves shut up in parishes, in our communities, in our parish or diocesan institutions, when so many people are waiting for the Gospel! To go out as ones sent. It is not enough simply to open the door in welcome because they come, but we must go out through that door to seek and meet the people.

— Homily, World Youth Day, July 27, 2013

Reflection: Pray that the Lord will lead you out of your comfort zone this week to bring his love to someone you meet. Then be ready to share a smile, an encouraging word, practical help, or whatever the situation calls for.

A Christian Can Never Be Sad!

A Christian can never be sad! Never give way to discouragement! Ours is not a joy born of having many possessions, but from having encountered a Person: Jesus, in our midst; it is born from knowing that with him we are never alone, even at difficult moments, even when our life's journey comes up against problems and obstacles that seem insurmountable, and there are so many of them! And in this moment, the enemy, the devil, comes, often disguised as an angel, and slyly speaks his word to us. Do not listen to him! Let us follow Jesus!

— Homily, March 23, 2013

Reflection: What obstacles are you facing right now? Look for Jesus' presence and listen for his voice in these situations. Ask him to lead you.

The Joy of Evangelization

Let us witness to the newness, hope, and joy that the Lord brings to life. Let us feel within us "the delightful and comforting joy of evangelizing" (Paul VI, apostolic exhortation *Evangelii Nuntiandi*, n. 80). Because evangelizing, proclaiming Jesus, gives us joy. Instead, egoism makes us bitter, sad, and depresses us. Evangelizing uplifts us.

— General Audience, May 22, 2013

Reflection: Have you ever experienced the joy of evangelizing? Give God a chance to speak through you.

Real-Life Christians

Are we open to the Holy Spirit? Do we let ourselves be guided by him? Christians are "spiritual." This does not mean that we are people who live "in the clouds," far removed from real life, as if it were some kind of mirage. No! The Christian is someone who thinks and acts in everyday life according to God's will, someone who allows his or her life to be guided and nourished by the Holy Spirit, to be a full life, a life worthy of true sons and daughters.

— Homily, June 16, 2013

Reflection: Do you invite the Holy Spirit into your life at the beginning of every day — and even throughout the day? How can the Holy Spirit play a role in your everyday reality?

Our Poverty

We all experience our poverty, our weakness in taking the precious treasure of the Gospel to the world, but we must constantly repeat St. Paul's words: "We have this treasure in earthen vessels, to show that the transcendent power belongs to God and not to us" (2 Corinthians 4:7). It is this that must always give us courage: knowing that the power of evangelization comes from God, that it belongs to him.

— Address, May 17, 2013

Reflection: What weakness of yours prevents you from sharing the faith? Take this moment to further place your trust in God.

Accepting Old Age

Sometimes it seems to me that, in our relationships with children and young people, we are like adults who abandon and disregard these little ones because they reveal our bitterness and our failure to accept old age. We abandon them to the vicissitudes of the street, with the attitude of "every man for himself." We abandon them to places of entertainment where they can amuse themselves. Or we abandon them to the care of the cold and passive anonymity of modern technologies.

We set aside our care for them, and we even imitate them because we do not want to accept our place as adults. We fail to understand that the commandment of love requires us to care, to set boundaries, to broaden horizons, and to give witness with our lives.

— *Only Love Can Save Us*, Homily, May 25, 2012

Reflection: What responsibilities has God given you? What can you do this week to be faithful to them? In what areas is God calling you to take on more responsibility?

Rend Your Hearts

The words of the prophet Joel are strong and challenging: Rend your hearts, and not your garments, and return to the Lord your God. These words are an invitation to all people; they exclude no one.

Rend your hearts and your garments of a penance that is not sincere and that does not guarantee an eternal future. Rend your hearts and not your garments of any fast that is merely a formality or an observance which only serves to make us feel satisfied. Rend your hearts and not your garments of superficial and self-centered prayer that does not reach the innermost being of your life so that God may touch it. Rend your hearts so that you may say along with the Psalmist, "We have sinned."

— *Only Love Can Save Us*, Lenten Message, February 13, 2013

Reflection: In the depth of your hearts, ask God for forgiveness. Ask him what you can do to center your life more on him.

Plastic Smiles

Lent comes to us with its shout of truth and hope. It tells us that we do not have to slap on makeup and draw plastic smiles as if nothing were happening....

God invites us to ... admit that something inside us is not well, and that something in society or in the Church is not well. He invites us to change, to turn around, and to be converted.

— *Only Love Can Save Us*, Lenten Message, February 13, 2013

Reflection: What aspect of your life needs conversion? Take one step forward in this area today.

Always the Cross

It is the Cross — always the Cross that is present with Christ, because at times we are offered the Cross without Christ: this has not purpose! — it is the Cross, and always the Cross with Christ, which guarantees the fruitfulness of our mission.

— Homily, Mass With Seminarians and Novices, July 7, 2013

Reflection: What cross is Jesus inviting you to carry this month?

Gratitude

Lent ... must be a time of conversion that flows out of gratitude for all that God has given us; for all that he has accomplished and will continue to accomplish in the world, in history and in our own personal lives. Our gratitude must be like Mary's, who, in spite of all the sorrows she had to endure, did not cast down her eyes in defeat, but instead sang of the greatness of the Lord.

— *Only Love Can Save Us*, Lenten Letter, February 22, 2012

Reflection: Write a list of ten things you are grateful for. Take time to thank God for each one.

To Meet Each Other

I sometimes ask people: "Do you give alms?" They say to me: "Yes, Father." "And when you give alms, do you look the person you are giving them to in the eye?" "Oh, I don't know, I don't really notice." "Then you have not really encountered him. You tossed him the alms and walked off. When you give alms, do you touch the person's hand or do you throw the coin?" "No, I throw the coin." "So you did not touch him. And if you don't touch him you don't meet him."

What Jesus teaches us first of all is to meet each other, and in meeting to offer each other help. We must know how to meet each other. We must build, create, construct a culture of encounter.

— Message, August 7, 2013

Reflection: How can you build this culture of encounter, especially in your care of the poor?

Where Are You?

This is the first question which God asks man after his sin. "Adam, where are you?" Adam lost his bearings, his place in creation, because he thought he could be powerful, able to control everything, to be God. Harmony was lost; man erred and this error occurs over and over again also in relationships with others. "The other" is no longer a brother or sister to be loved, but simply someone who disturbs my life and my comfort.

— Homily, July 8, 2013

Reflection: Who disturbs your life? How can you respond in love?

God Is Pure Mercy

"Put on Christ": he awaits you in the sacrament of Penance, with his mercy he will cure all the wounds caused by sin. Do not be afraid to ask God's forgiveness, because he never tires of forgiving us, like a father who loves us. God is pure mercy!

— Address, World Youth Day, July 25, 2013

Reflection: When was the last time you participated in the sacrament of Penance? Find a time to go this week.

Glorified on the Cross

But difficulties and trials are part of the path that leads to God's glory, just as they were for Jesus, who was glorified on the Cross; we will always encounter them in life! Do not be discouraged! We have the power of the Holy Spirit to overcome these trials!

— Homily, April 28, 2013

Reflection: Consider how you can unite your difficulties and trials to Jesus' suffering and death on the Cross.

This Is the Path

If we want to take the path of worldliness, bargaining with the world … we will never have the consolation of the Lord. And if we seek consolation alone, it will be a superficial consolation, not the Lord's consolation, but a human consolation.

The Church always advances between the cross and the resurrection, between persecutions and the consolations of the Lord. This is the path: those who take this path do not go wrong.

— Homily, April 23, 2013

Reflection: What situations in your life cause you to choose the path of worldliness? Take some time to place your trust more deeply in the Lord's consolation.

A Response to Evil

The Cross is the word through which God has responded to evil in the world. Sometimes it may seem as though God does not react to evil, as if he is silent. And yet, God has spoken, he has replied, and his answer is the Cross of Christ: a word which is love, mercy, forgiveness.

— Address, March 29, 2013

Reflection: Do you sometimes wonder where God is when you see evil in the world? Remember to think about Jesus' gift on the Cross when these situations arise.

Entering Into Death

What has the Cross given to those who have gazed upon it and to those who have touched it? What has the Cross left in each one of us? You see, it gives us a treasure that no one else can give: the certainty of the faithful love which God has for us. A love so great that it enters into our sin and forgives it, enters into our suffering and gives us the strength to bear it.

It is a love which enters into death to conquer it and to save us.

— Address, World Youth Day, Way of the Cross, July 26, 2013

Reflection: Meditate on the Stations of the Cross. Ponder the treasure that God has given to you.

Talk, Talk, Talk.... No!

My experience is what I feel in front of the tabernacle, when I go in the evening to pray before the Lord. Sometimes I nod off for a while; this is true, for the strain of the day more or less makes you fall asleep, but he understands. I feel great comfort when I think of the Lord looking at me. We think we have to pray and talk, talk, talk.... No! Let the Lord look at you. When he looks at us, he gives us strength and helps us to bear witness to him.

— Address, May 18, 2013

Reflection: Take at least five minutes right now to be silent before God.

No Longer Attentive

How many of us, myself included, have lost our bearings; we are no longer attentive to the world in which we live; we don't care; we don't protect what God created for everyone, and we end up unable even to care for one another!

— Homily, July 8, 2013

Reflection: Where has our culture gone wrong in caring for one another? Where have you taken on some of this culture in your own life?

The Gift of Hope

For us Christians, wherever the Cross is, there is hope, always. If there is no hope, we are not Christian. That is why I like to say: do not allow yourselves to be robbed of hope. May we not be robbed of hope, because this strength is a grace, a gift from God which carries us forward with our eyes fixed on heaven.

— Homily, August 15, 2013

Reflection: What robs you of hope? Ask God for the gift of hope in your life.

Think of St. Joseph

Let us think of St. Joseph, who watched over Mary and Jesus, of his care for the family God had entrusted to him, and of the attentive gaze with which he guided it to avoid the perils on the way. For this reason, may pastors know how to be in front of the flock to show it the way, in the midst of the flock to keep it united, and behind the flock to prevent anyone from being left behind and because the flock itself has, so to speak, a "good nose" for finding the way. This is how the pastor must move!

— Address, June 21, 2013

Reflection: St. Joseph is a great model for all of us as we care for and protect the people in our lives. What can we learn from his example of uncomplaining obedience to God's call and his wholehearted readiness to serve?

Freely Given

When Jesus sent his disciples to proclaim the Kingdom, he told them, "Freely you have received; freely give" (Matthew 10:8, NIV). The Lord wants his kingdom to be spread through gestures of love freely given. This is how men and women recognized the first Christians as they went about spreading the message that overflowed from them. "Freely you have received, freely give." . . . The Church grows by attraction, by its witness, not by proselytism.

— *Only Love Can Save Us*, Lenten Letter, February 22, 2012

Reflection: Keeping in mind God's gifts to us, what gestures of love and encouragement can you freely give to others? How can you live with this perspective today?

A Scandal

Faith in Jesus Christ is not a joke; it is something very serious. It is a scandal that God came to be one of us. It is a scandal that he died on a cross. It is a scandal: the scandal of the Cross. The Cross continues to provoke scandal. But it is the one sure path, the path of the Cross, the path of Jesus, the path of the Incarnation of Jesus.

Please do not water down your faith in Jesus Christ. We dilute fruit drinks — orange, apple, or banana juice, but please do not drink a diluted form of faith.

— Address, World Youth Day, July 25, 2013

Reflection: In what ways do you water down your faith in Jesus? Meditate on the Cross to help you strengthen your commitment to him.

Bite Your Tongue!

Let each one ask him- or herself today: "Do I increase harmony in my family, in my parish, in my community, or am I a gossip? Am I a cause of division or embarrassment?" And you know the harm that gossiping does to the Church, to the parishes, the communities. Gossip does harm! Gossip wounds.

Before Christians open their mouths to gossip, they should bite their tongues! To bite one's tongue: this does us good because the tongue swells and can no longer speak, cannot gossip. "Am I humble enough to patiently stitch up, through sacrifice, the open wounds in communion?"

— General Audience, September 25, 2013

Reflection: Do you know of a situation where you need to bite your tongue? Ask the Lord for the grace to avoid gossip and to speak well of others.

Only Love Can Save Us

We already know where the voracious greed for power, the imposition of one's ideas as absolute, and the rejection of those who think differently will take us: to a numbness of conscience and to abandonment. Only the commandment of love in all its simplicity — steady, humble, unassuming but firm in conviction and in commitment to others — can save us.

— *Only Love Can Save Us*, Homily, May 25, 2012

Reflection: Why do you think humility is essential to love? How might a spirit of humility help you to love others more wholeheartedly and realistically?

The Bitterness the Devil Offers

Let us never yield to pessimism, to that bitterness that the devil offers us every day; let us not yield to pessimism or discouragement: let us be quite certain that the Holy Spirit bestows upon the Church, with his powerful breath, the courage to persevere and also to seek new methods of evangelization, so as to bring the Gospel to the uttermost ends of the earth (cf. Acts1:8).

— Address, March 15, 2013

Reflection: What makes you pessimistic about yourself, your Church, and your world? Ask the Holy Spirit to give you hope and courage.

Relive Her "Yes"

In this regard, we must learn from Mary, we must relive her "yes," her unreserved readiness to receive the Son of God in her life, which was transformed from that moment. Through the Holy Spirit, the Father and the Son take up their abode with us: we live in God and of God. Yet is our life truly inspired by God? How many things do I put before God?

— General Audience, May 15, 2013

Reflection: What do you put before God? How can you relive Mary's "yes" to what God wants for you?

Never Give Up

Dear brothers and sisters, let us not be closed to the newness that God wants to bring into our lives! Are we often weary, disheartened, and sad? Do we feel weighed down by our sins? Do we think that we won't be able to cope? Let us not close our hearts, let us not lose confidence, let us never give up: there are no situations which God cannot change, there is no sin which he cannot forgive if only we open ourselves to him.

— Homily, Easter Vigil, March 30, 2013

Reflection: What new things is God doing in your life? How can you open yourself up more to what he wants from you?

The Nakedness of His Sin

Adam, after his sin, experiences shame, he feels naked, he senses the weight of what he has done; and yet God does not abandon him.... God immediately asks: "Adam, where are you?" He seeks him out. Jesus took on our nakedness, he took upon himself the shame of Adam, the nakedness of his sin, in order to wash away our sin: by his wounds we have been healed.

— Homily, Divine Mercy Sunday, April 7, 2013

Reflection: Take some time to reflect on your sins and Jesus' gift on the Cross. Allow yourself to experience his healing.

To Be Crucified Again

According to an ancient Roman tradition, while fleeing the city during the persecutions of Nero, St. Peter saw Jesus, who was traveling in the opposite direction — that is, toward the city — and asked him in amazement: "Lord, where are you going?" Jesus' response was: "I am going to Rome to be crucified again." At that moment, Peter understood that he had to follow the Lord with courage, to the very end. But he also realized that he would never be alone on the journey; Jesus, who had loved him even unto death, would always be with him.

— Address, World Youth Day, July 26, 2013

Reflection: How do you identify with Peter? How is God with you on the journey?

The First Reform

The Church's ministers must be merciful, take responsibility for the people, and accompany them like the good Samaritan, who washes, cleans, and raises up his neighbor. This is pure Gospel. God is greater than sin. The structural and organizational reforms are secondary — that is, they come afterward. The first reform must be the attitude.

The ministers of the Gospel must be people who can warm the hearts of the people, who walk through the dark night with them, who know how to dialogue and to descend themselves into their people's night, into the darkness, but without getting lost.

— Interview With Pope Francis, *America* magazine,
September 30, 2013

Reflection: Think of someone you admire who is great at "walking with" others, at extending compassion. How can you follow that example? What steps can you take to overcome any indifference you might feel?

Final Decision

Dear brothers and sisters, how difficult it is [to] take a final decision in our time. Temporary things seduce us. We are victims of a trend that pushes us to the provisional ... as though we wanted to stay adolescents. There is a little charm in staying adolescents, and this for life!

Let us not be afraid of life commitments, commitments that take up and concern our entire life! In this way, our life will be fruitful! And this is freedom: to have the courage to make these decisions with generosity.

— Address, May 4, 2013

Reflection: What decisions are you currently avoiding? Ask God to help you make a decision today.

God Likes You

And we, do we listen to the Holy Spirit? What does the Holy Spirit tell us? He says: God loves you. He tells us this. God loves you, God likes you. Do we truly love God and others, as Jesus does?

Let us allow ourselves to be guided by the Holy Spirit, let us allow him to speak to our heart and say this to us: God is love, God is waiting for us, God is Father, he loves us as a true father loves, he loves us truly, and only the Holy Spirit can tell us this in our hearts.

— General Audience, May 8, 2013

Reflection: In your heart, reflect on how you view God. Ask the Holy Spirit to help you understand God's love for you.

"You Fool!"

[At times] we want to save ourselves, and we believe that we can. Maybe we don't exactly say it, but that's how we live. [For example] when we think, "I can save myself with money. I am secure, I have some money, there is no problem. . . . I have dignity: the dignity of being rich."

. . . Think of the Gospel parable, of that man who had the full granary and said: "I will make another, to have more and more, and then I will sleep peacefully." And the Lord responds: "You fool! You will die tonight." That kind of salvation is wrong, it is temporary, apparent.

— Homily, Domus Sanctae Marthae, April 10, 2013

Reflection: How does the way you live demonstrate where you've placed your hope for salvation? In the world? In riches? In power? Place your trust in a salvation that only comes from Jesus' death on the Cross.

We Have Lost the Ninety-Nine!

I want to tell you something. There is a beautiful passage of the Gospel which tells us about the shepherd who, when he returned to the sheepfold, realized that one sheep was missing. He left the ninety-nine others and went in search of it; he went off to look for one. But brothers and sisters, we have one sheep. We have lost the other ninety-nine! We must go out, we must go out to them! In this culture — let us tell the truth — we only have one; we are a minority! And do we feel the fervor, the apostolic zeal to go out and find the other ninety-nine?

This is an enormous responsibility and we must ask the Lord for the grace of generosity, and the courage and patience to go out, to go out and preach the Gospel. Ah, this is difficult. It is easier to stay at home, with that one sheep! It is easier with that sheep to comb its fleece, to stroke it … but we priests and you Christians too, everyone: the Lord wants us to be shepherds, he does not want us to fuss with combing fleeces! Shepherds!

— Address, June 17, 2013

Reflection: Jesus is asking you to go out and get the ninety-nine. How do you feel about this? What do you fear? What are your hopes? Talk to the Lord about this, and ask for the generosity you will need.

Forgotten How to Weep

We are a society which has forgotten how to weep, how to experience compassion — "suffering with" others: the globalization of indifference has taken from us the ability to weep! ... [L]et us ask the Lord for the grace to weep over our indifference, to weep over the cruelty of our world, of our own hearts, and of all those who in anonymity make social and economic decisions which open the door to tragic situations.... Today has anyone wept in our world?

— Homily, July 8, 2013

Reflection: Take a moment to examine your compassion for others, those around you and those in the world. What can you do to help others in concrete ways in the next couple of weeks?

Sign of Love

Let us open the doors to the Spirit, let ourselves be guided by him, and allow God's constant help to make us new men and women, inspired by the love of God, which the Holy Spirit bestows on us! How beautiful it would be if each of you, every evening, could say: Today at school, at home, at work, guided by God, I showed a sign of love toward one of my friends, my parents, an older person! How beautiful!

— Homily, Holy Mass of Confirmation, April 28, 2013

Reflection: Try to live out Pope Francis' words in an intentional way today. Ask the Holy Spirit to provide opportunities for you to show signs of love toward someone, not only today but every day.

Lights of Hope

The one with the upper hand is God, and God is our hope! It is true that nowadays, to some extent, everyone, including our young people, feels attracted by the many idols which take the place of God and appear to offer hope: money, success, power, pleasure. Often a growing sense of loneliness and emptiness in the hearts of many people leads them to seek satisfaction in these ephemeral idols.

Dear brothers and sisters, let us be lights of hope! Let us maintain a positive outlook on reality.

— Homily, World Youth Day, July 24, 2013

Reflection: Make additional time for a young person in your life this week. Be a light of hope.

The Church's Credibility

Let us all remember this: One cannot proclaim the Gospel of Jesus without the tangible witness of one's life. Those who listen to us and observe us must be able to see in our actions what they hear from our lips, and so give glory to God!

... Inconsistency on the part of pastors and the faithful between what they say and what they do, between word and manner of life, is undermining the Church's credibility.

— Homily, April 14, 2013

Reflection: What aspect of your life harms your witness to the Church's credibility?

He Walks at Our Pace

There is no "set protocol" for God's action in our life ... it does not exist. He intervenes in one way, later in another, but he always intervenes. The Lord always chooses his way to enter into our lives. Often he does so slowly, so slowly that we are in danger of losing our patience a little. But Lord, when?

... The Lord takes his time. But even he, in this relationship with us, has a lot of patience. He waits for us! And he waits for us until the end of life! Think of the good thief, right at the end, at the very end, he acknowledged God. The Lord walks with us, but often does not reveal himself, as in the case of the disciples of Emmaus.

The Lord is involved in our lives — that's for sure! — but often we do not see. This demands our patience. But the Lord who walks with us, he also has a lot of patience with us ... [and] walks at our pace.

— Homily, Domus Sanctae Marthae, June 28, 2013

Reflection: Where are you being patient with the Lord? Where is he being patient with you?

Robbing the Poor

In this sense, I encourage the financial experts and the political leaders of your countries to consider the words of St. John Chrysostom: "Not to share one's goods with the poor is to rob them and to deprive them of life. It is not our goods that we possess, but theirs" (*Homily on Lazarus*, 1:6 — PG 48, 992D).

— Address, May 16, 2013

Reflection: How can you see money as a way to bless others? What is God asking you to do with the gifts and resources he has given you?

Permeated

The spread of the Gospel is not guaranteed either by the number of persons, or by the prestige of the institution, or by the quantity of available resources. What counts is to be permeated by the love of Christ, to let oneself be led by the Holy Spirit and to graft one's own life onto the tree of life, which is the Lord's Cross.

— Homily, Mass With Seminarians and Novices, July 7, 2013

Reflection: Place your trust in him. He will help you spread the Gospel.

Good for the Heart

Remain steadfast in the journey of faith, with firm hope in the Lord. This is the secret of our journey! He gives us the courage to swim against the tide. Pay attention ... to go against the current; this is good for the heart, but we need courage to swim against the tide. Jesus gives us this courage!

— Homily, Holy Mass of Confirmation, April 28, 2013

Reflection: Today's culture is a very strong tide. Are there any negative aspects of the culture that are particularly hard for you to resist? Where do you need courage in your journey of faith?

Let Us Go to Jesus

Let us not forget that the Lord always watches over us with mercy; he always watches over us with mercy. Let us not be afraid of approaching him! He has a merciful heart! If we show him our inner wounds, our inner sins, he will always forgive us. It is pure mercy. Let us go to Jesus!

— Angelus address, June 9, 2013

Reflection: Examine your life and talk to God about your inner wounds. Find a time to go to confession this week.

Not Just in Books

Some people will say, "No, I prefer to read about faith in books!" It is important to read about faith, but look, on its own this is not enough! What is important is our encounter with Jesus, our encounter with him, and this is what gives you faith because he is the one who gives it to you!

— Address, May 18, 2013

Reflection: How can you encounter God this week, through deep conversation with God and through others?

Holding Nothing Back

In Holy Week, we live the crowning moment of this journey, of this plan of love that runs through the entire history of the relations between God and humanity. Jesus enters Jerusalem to take his last step with which he sums up the whole of his existence. He gives himself without reserve; he keeps nothing for himself, not even life.

— General Audience, March 27, 2013

Reflection: Take some time to read and think about the love of God made known to us through the self-emptying of Jesus on the Cross.

Staying With Jesus

The logic of the Cross ... is not primarily that of suffering and death, but rather that of love and of the gift of self which brings life.... Following and accompanying Christ, staying with him, demands "coming out of ourselves," requires us to be outgoing; to come out of ourselves, out of a dreary way of living faith that has become a habit, out of the temptation to withdraw into our own plans, which end by shutting out God's creative action.

— General Audience, March 27, 2013

Reflection: How are you "accompanying Christ" this week? Ask God to change your logic into the logic of the Cross and to bring you out of a faith that is merely habit.

You Do Not Carry Your Cross Alone!

The Cross of Christ bears the suffering and the sin of mankind, including our own. Jesus accepts all this with open arms, bearing on his shoulders our crosses and saying to us: "Have courage! You do not carry your cross alone! I carry it with you. I have overcome death and I have come to give you hope, to give you life" (cf. John 3:16).

— Address, World Youth Day, Way of the Cross, July 26, 2013

Reflection: What are you worried about today? Make a list and give these things over to Jesus, who carries these burdens with you.

Praying to the Devil

When we do not profess Jesus Christ, the saying of Léon Bloy comes to mind: "Anyone who does not pray to the Lord prays to the devil." When we do not profess Jesus Christ, we profess the worldliness of the devil, a demonic worldliness.

— Homily, March 14, 2013

Reflection: Professing Jesus means professing Jesus as Lord in your heart, with your words, and with your actions. Take time this week to profess Jesus as Lord in all these areas.

All for Us

At the Last Supper, with his friends, he breaks the bread and passes the cup round "for us." The Son of God offers himself to us; he puts his Body and his Blood into our hands, so as to be with us always, to dwell among us. And in the Garden of Olives, and likewise in the trial before Pilate, he puts up no resistance, he gives himself; he is the suffering Servant, foretold by Isaiah, who empties himself, even unto death (cf. Isaiah 53:12).

— General Audience, March 27, 2013

Reflection: Take some extra time after Mass to thank God for the great gift of the Eucharist!

He Gave Himself Up for You

Jesus gave himself up to death voluntarily in order to reciprocate the love of God the Father, in perfect union with his will, to demonstrate his love for us. On the Cross, Jesus "loved me and gave himself for me" (Galatians 2:20). Each one of us can say: "He loved me and gave himself for me." Each one can say this "for me."

— General Audience, March 27, 2013

Reflection: Spend some time considering that Jesus died specifically for you.

Who Do You Want to Be?

But the Cross of Christ invites us also to allow ourselves to be smitten by his love, teaching us always to look upon others with mercy and tenderness, especially those who suffer, who are in need of help, who need a word or a concrete action.... How many times have we seen them in the Way of the Cross, how many times have they accompanied Jesus on the way to Calvary: Pilate, Simon of Cyrene, Mary, the women....

And you, who do you want to be? Like Pilate? Like Simon? Like Mary? Jesus is looking at you now and is asking you: Do you want to help me carry the Cross? Brothers and sisters, with all the strength of your youth, how will you respond to him?

— Address, World Youth Day, Way of the Cross, July 26, 2013

Reflection: Think about all of the characters on the journey to Calvary. Which one are you most like? Which one do you want to be?

Let Us Feel the Joy!

At dawn, they went to the tomb to anoint Jesus' body and found the first sign: the empty tomb (cf. Mark 16:1). Their meeting with a messenger of God followed. He announced: "Jesus of Nazareth, the Crucified One, has risen, he is not here" (cf. vv. 5-6). The women were motivated by love and were able to accept this announcement with faith: they believed and passed it on straight away; they did not keep it to themselves but passed it on....

This should happen in our lives too. Let us feel the joy of being Christian! We believe in the Risen One who conquered evil and death! Let us have the courage to "come out of ourselves" to take this joy and this light to all the places of our life!

— General Audience, April 3, 2013

Reflection: Where do you find joy? Ask God to help you make Jesus' new life the center of your joy.

A New Condition

Jesus makes himself present in a new way, he is the Crucified One, but his body is glorified; he did not return to earthly life but returned in a new condition. . . . For us, too, there are many signs through which the Risen One makes himself known: Sacred Scripture, the Eucharist, the other sacraments, charity, all those acts of love which bring a ray of the Risen One.

Let us permit ourselves to be illuminated by Christ's resurrection, let him transform us with his power, so that through us too, the signs of death may give way to signs of life in the world.

— General Audience, April 3, 2013

Reflection: What's one concrete way for you to know the Risen One better? Take time this week to further your commitment to Scripture, the Eucharist, or an act of charity.

The Foundation of Our Faith

What does the Resurrection mean for our life? And why is our faith in vain without it? Our faith is founded on Christ's death and resurrection, just as a house stands on its foundations: if they give way, the whole house collapses.

Jesus gave himself on the Cross, taking the burden of our sins upon himself and descending into the abyss of death; then in the Resurrection, he triumphed over them, took them away, and opened before us the path to rebirth and to a new life.

— General Audience, April 10, 2013

Reflection: Would your life be any different without the Resurrection? Reflect on what it means for your life and how your actions flow from this great gift?

Are You a Revolutionary?

There have been so many revolutionaries in history, many indeed. Yet none of them have had the force of this revolution which brought Jesus to us: a revolution to transform history, a revolution that changes the human heart in depth. The revolutions of history have changed political and economic systems, but none have really changed the human heart.

True revolution, the revolution that radically transforms life was brought about by Jesus Christ through his resurrection.... In this day and age, unless Christians are revolutionaries, they are not Christians.

— Address, June 17, 2013

Reflection: Are you a revolutionary? How can you trust in God for a more radical transformation of your life?

The Victory of Christ

The grace contained in the sacraments of Easter is an enormous potential for the renewal of our personal existence, of family life, of social relations. However, everything passes through the human heart: if I let myself be touched by the grace of the Risen Christ, if I let him change me in that aspect of mine which is not good, which can hurt me and others, I allow the victory of Christ to be affirmed in my life.

— *Regina Caeli* address, April 1, 2013

Reflection: How can you receive the graces of the sacraments more effectively? Look for an article or a book that will help you learn more about how the Lord can lead, heal, and strengthen you through the sacraments.

How Do You Know If You Truly Know Jesus?

This history of the first Christian community tells us something very important which applies to the Church in all times and also to us. When a person truly knows Jesus Christ and believes in him, that person experiences his presence in life as well as the power of his resurrection, and cannot but communicate this experience.

— *Regina Caeli* address, April 14, 2013

Reflection: Are you able to communicate the presence of Jesus in your life? What do you need to do to more truly know Jesus Christ?

That Is Where Death Is

Our daily problems and worries can wrap us up in ourselves, in sadness and bitterness ... and that is where death is. That is not the place to look for the One who is alive! Let the risen Jesus enter your life; welcome him as a friend, with trust: he is life!

— Homily, Easter Vigil, March 30, 2013

Reflection: Invite Jesus into your problems and fears. Expect him to show up.

The Lord's Most Powerful Message

I think we, too, are the people who, on the one hand, want to listen to Jesus, but on the other hand, at times, like to find a stick to beat others with, to condemn others. And Jesus has this message for us: mercy.

I think — and I say it with humility — that this is the Lord's most powerful message: mercy.

— Homily, March 17, 2013

Reflection: Where do you need to experience God's mercy, patience, and forgiveness? To whom do you need to be merciful?

Joy and Fervor

I make my own the words of Paul VI, which are as timely as if they had been written yesterday.... "[M]ay the world of our time, which is searching, sometimes with anguish, sometimes with hope, be enabled to receive the Good News not from evangelizers who are dejected, discouraged, impatient or anxious, but from ministers of the Gospel whose lives glow with fervor, who have first received the joy of Christ, and who are willing to risk their lives so that the Kingdom of God may be proclaimed and the Church established in the midst of the world" (cf. apostolic letter *Evangelii Nuntiandi*, n. 80).

— Address, May 17, 2013

Reflection: How can you reject impatience and anxiety and restore joy and fervor in your life? How would this transformation improve your witness to others?

Our Strength

It is the Resurrection itself that opens us to greater hope, for it opens our life and the life of the world to the eternal future of God, to full happiness, to the certainty that evil, sin, and death may be overcome. And this leads to living daily situations with greater trust, to facing them with courage and determination.

Christ's resurrection illuminates these everyday situations with a new light. The Resurrection of Christ is our strength!

— General Audience, April 3, 2013

Reflection: How does the Resurrection change your perspective toward your everyday situations?

The Living Water

At this point, we may ask ourselves: Why can this water quench our thirst deep down? We know that water is essential to life; without water, we die; it quenches, washes, makes the earth fertile. In the Letter to the Romans, we find these words: "God's love has been poured into our hearts through the Holy Spirit who has been given to us" (5:5). The "living water," the Holy Spirit, the Gift of the Risen One who dwells in us, purifies us, illuminates us, renews us, transforms us, because he makes us participants in the very life of God that is Love.

— General Audience, May 8, 2013

Reflection: What do you thirst for in life? How can you allow Jesus to quench this thirst?

Work Fills Us With Dignity

FEAST OF ST. JOSEPH THE WORKER

Work is part of God's loving plan; we are called to cultivate and care for all the goods of creation and in this way share in the work of creation! Work is fundamental to the dignity of a person. Work, to use a metaphor, "anoints" us with dignity, fills us with dignity, makes us similar to God, who has worked and still works, who always acts (cf. John 5:17); it gives one the ability to maintain oneself, one's family, to contribute to the growth of one's own nation.

— General Audience, May 1, 2013

Reflection: How does work bring meaning to your life? Where in your work can you find God? Reflect on how you can grow closer to God through the people you work with and the job that you do.

Free for Goodness

First of all: Be free people! What do I mean? ... Freedom means being able to think about what we do, being able to assess what is good and what is bad — these are the types of conduct that lead to development; it means always opting for the good. Let us be free for goodness. And in this, do not be afraid to go against the tide, even if it is not easy! Always being free to choose goodness is demanding, but it will make you into people with a backbone who can face life, people with courage and patience.

— Address, To the Students of the Jesuit Schools
of Italy and Albania, June 6, 2013

Reflection: Are you free to make the right choices in life, despite the culture? Where do you need to have a stronger backbone?

Help My Unbelief

Maybe someone among us here is thinking: My sin is so great, I am as far from God as the younger son in the parable, my unbelief is like that of Thomas; I don't have the courage to go back, to believe that God can welcome me and that he is waiting for me, of all people. But God is indeed waiting for you; he asks of you only the courage to go to him.

— Homily, Divine Mercy Sunday, April 7, 2013

Reflection: Speak to God about your sins and doubts. Be honest with him about how you think and feel. Do not be afraid. Pray like the father in Mark's Gospel, "I believe; help my unbelief!" (Mark 9:24).

The Sheep Know the Shepherd

The sheep know the voice of their shepherd and recognize who he is. They know who the shepherd is, and they know who is not. They know who is a mercenary. They know who, when the wolf comes, is going to defend them and who's going to take off. They know this. For this reason, Jesus says, "My sheep hear my voice, and I know them, and they follow me" (John 10:27).

— *Only Love Can Save Us*, Homily, August 4, 2006

Reflection: What voices do you trust? How do the opinions of others affect the way you live? Take some time to place your trust in Jesus' voice. Let his voice in the Gospels be the strongest voice in your life.

Strong, Safe, and Sound

The Risen Lord is the hope that never fails, that never disappoints (cf. Romans 5:5). Hope does not let us down — the hope of the Lord! How often in our life do hopes vanish, how often do the expectations we have in our heart come to nothing! Our hope as Christians is strong, safe and sound on this earth, where God has called us to walk, and it is open to eternity because it is founded on God, who is always faithful. We must not forget: God is always faithful to us.

— General Audience, April 10, 2013

Reflection: In the past, what hopes have disappointed you? How is hope in Jesus different? How can this perspective change the way you live?

Everything Is Different

You see how faith accomplishes a revolution in us, one which we can call Copernican; it removes us from the center and puts God at the center; faith immerses us in his love and gives us security, strength, and hope. Seemingly, nothing has changed; yet, in the depths of our being, everything is different. With God, peace, consolation, gentleness, courage, serenity, and joy, which are all fruits of the Holy Spirit (cf. Galatians 5:22), find a home in our heart; then our very being is transformed; our way of thinking and acting is made new, it becomes Jesus' own, God's own, way of thinking and acting. Dear friends, faith is revolutionary and today I ask you: Are you open to entering into this revolutionary wave of faith? Only by entering into this wave will your young lives make sense and so be fruitful!

— Address, World Youth Day, July 25, 2013

Reflection: Have you put God at the very center of your life? Are you open to this "revolutionary wave of faith"? If you have put God at the center, what fruit does he bear in your life?

God of Today

Jesus no longer belongs to the past but lives in the present and is projected toward the future; Jesus is the everlasting "today" of God.

— Homily, Easter Vigil, March 30, 2013

Reflection: What does it mean to live in the present with God? How is he calling you to love him today? What can you do today to remain close to him in the future?

Ready to Embrace Us

God is patient with us because he loves us, and those who love are able to understand, to hope, to inspire confidence; they do not give up, they do not burn bridges, they are able to forgive.

Let us remember this in our lives as Christians: God always waits for us, even when we have left him behind! He is never far from us, and if we return to him, he is ready to embrace us.

— Homily, Divine Mercy Sunday, April 7, 2013

Reflection: In the silence of your heart, recollect that God is very near to you. In what ways is he asking you to return to him?

With His Flesh

When Jesus healed a sick man, he was not only a healer. When he taught people — let us think of the Beatitudes — he was not only a catechist, a preacher of morals. When he remonstrated against the hypocrisy of the Pharisees and Sadducees, he was not a revolutionary who wanted to drive out the Romans. No, these things that Jesus did — healing, teaching, and speaking out against hypocrisy — were only a sign of something greater that Jesus was doing: he was forgiving sins.... Everything else — healing, teaching, reprimands — are only signs of that deeper miracle which is the re-creation of the world.

Thus, reconciliation is the re-creation of the world; and the most profound mission of Jesus is the redemption of all of us sinners. And Jesus did not do this with words, with actions, or by walking on the road, no! He did it with his flesh. It is truly he, God, who becomes one of us, a man, to heal us from within.

— Homily, Domus Sanctae Marthae, July 4, 2013

Reflection: Sin leaves us wounded, but Jesus has the power to recreate our hearts through the forgiveness of sins. He doesn't forgive us from far away. He is not distant. He is near you now and wants you to draw closer to him to be healed. How will you respond?

Is It Possible to Walk
the Path of Peace?

And at this point I ask myself: Is it possible to walk the path of peace? Can we get out of this spiral of sorrow and death? Can we learn once again to walk and live in the ways of peace? Invoking the help of God, under the maternal gaze of the Salus Populi Romani, Queen of Peace, I say: Yes, it is possible for everyone! From every corner of the world tonight, I would like to hear us cry out: Yes, it is possible for everyone! Or even better, I would like for each one of us, from the least to the greatest, including those called to govern nations, to respond: Yes, we want it!

My Christian faith urges me to look to the Cross. How I wish that all men and women of goodwill would look to the Cross if only for a moment! There, we can see God's reply: Violence is not answered with violence; death is not answered with the language of death.

— Vigil of Prayer for Peace, September 7, 2013

Reflection: In light of Christ's example on the Cross, how can you respond to the violence and evil around us?

Our Lady Is the One Who Knows Everything

Think about it: When we are too self-confident, we are more fragile — much more fragile. Always with the Lord, with the Lord! And when we say "with the Lord," we mean with the Eucharist, with the Bible, with prayer ... but also with the family, with our mother, also with her, because she is the one who brings us to the Lord; she is the mother, she is the one who knows everything.

— Address, Vigil of Pentecost With the Ecclesial Movements, May 18, 2013

Reflection: Take some time to reflect in gratitude on what you have been given from your own mother and from others who have cared for you. How can this perspective give you humility? How can this humility open you to more growth with the Lord?

Never Tire

I would like to make an appeal to those in possession of greater resources, to public authorities and to all people of goodwill who are working for social justice: Never tire of working for a more just world, marked by greater solidarity! No one can remain insensitive to the inequalities that persist in the world! Everybody, according to his or her particular opportunities and responsibilities, should be able to make a personal contribution to putting an end to so many social injustices.

— Address, World Youth Day, July 25, 2013

Reflection: What opportunities and responsibilities do you have to make a personal contribution to overcoming social injustices? What can you do in your community and in your situation?

Called by Name

FEAST OF OUR LADY OF FÁTIMA

Dear brothers and sisters, God calls us, by name and surname, each one of us, to proclaim the Gospel and to promote the culture of encounter with joy. The Virgin Mary is our exemplar.... Watch over me, Mother, when I am disoriented, and lead me by the hand. May you spur us on to meet our many brothers and sisters who are on the outskirts, who are hungry for God but have no one to proclaim him.

— Homily, World Youth Day, July 27, 2013

Reflection: God is calling you by name to be a missionary in your everyday life. With the gifts he has given you, where is he calling you to proclaim the Gospel?

Simple People

FEAST OF ST. MATTHIAS

Let us not forget that the apostles were simple people; they were neither scribes nor doctors of the law, nor did they belong to the class of priests. With their limitations and with the authorities against them, how did they manage to fill Jerusalem with their teaching (cf. Acts 5:28)? It is clear that only the presence with them of the Risen Lord and the action of the Holy Spirit can explain this fact.

— *Regina Caeli* address, April 14, 2013

Reflection: Throughout Scripture and the history of the Church, the Lord uses the lowly, the insignificant, and the sinful for his plans. Ask God to help you overcome your limitations and weaknesses so that you can serve him freely and confidently.

He Never Disappoints Anyone

The Cross of Christ contains all the love of God; there we find his immeasurable mercy. This is a love in which we can place all our trust, in which we can believe.... [L]et us entrust ourselves to Jesus, let us give ourselves over to him (cf. *Lumen Fidei*, n. 16), because he never disappoints anyone! Only in Christ crucified and risen can we find salvation and redemption.

— Address, World Youth Day, Way of the Cross, July 26, 2013

Reflection: Take a moment to entrust your life to Jesus in the depths of your heart. Think about the times you trust money, relationships, or power more than him. Give those temptations over to the Lord.

Not a Terminal Treatment

[Christian life is not] a terminal treatment to keep us quiet until we go to heaven.... Christian peace is a restive, not a torpid peace.... [It] impels us, and this is the beginning, the root of apostolic zeal. The love of Christ possesses us, impels us, urges us on with the emotion we feel when we see that God loves us.

— Homily, Domus Sanctae Marthae, June 15, 2013

Reflection: What emotions do you feel when you consider God's love for you? What role do your emotions play in enlivening your faith and making you a more proactive witness? If you feel little of his love or are burdened and weary, ask God to console you.

Unreserved Readiness

We are called to open ourselves more and more to the action of the Holy Spirit, to offer our unreserved readiness to be instruments of God's mercy, of his tenderness, of his love for every man and every woman and especially for the poor, the outcast, and those who are distant.

— Address, May 17, 2013

Reflection: What does it mean for you to open yourself more and more to the action of the Holy Spirit? How can you develop a heart of "unreserved readiness"? Ask Jesus to help you understand his mercy, and give it to others.

Trust in God's Work

There are no difficulties, trials, or misunderstandings to fear, provided we remain united to God as branches to the vine, provided we do not lose our friendship with him, provided we make ever more room for him in our lives. This is especially so whenever we feel poor, weak, and sinful, because God grants strength to our weakness, riches to our poverty, conversion and forgiveness to our sinfulness.

The Lord is so rich in mercy: every time, if we go to him, he forgives us. Let us trust in God's work!

— Homily, Holy Mass of Confirmation, April 28, 2013

Reflection: Think about the last time you faced a trial or difficulty. What can you do to unite yourself more to Jesus next time one occurs?

Culture of the Temporary

I heard a seminarian, a good seminarian, who said that he wanted to serve Christ for ten years, and then he would think about starting a different life.... This is dangerous! However, listen carefully: We are all, even the older people among us, we, too, are under pressure from this "culture of the temporary"; and this is dangerous because one does not put one's stakes on life once and for all. I marry as long as love lasts; I become a woman religious, but only for "a little while," "a short time," and then I shall see; I become a seminarian in order to become a priest, but I don't know how the story will end.

This is not right with Jesus! I am not reproaching you, I reproach this culture of the temporary, which hits us all, since it does us no good: because it is very hard today to make a definitive decision.

— Address, To Seminarians and Novices, July 6, 2013

Reflection: Where do you see the "culture of the temporary" in others around you? Where do you see it in yourself? In what specific ways could this attitude undermine your commitments?

How Do You Live the Eucharist?

The Eucharist is the sacrament of communion that brings us out of individualism so that we may follow him together, living out our faith in him. Therefore we should all ask ourselves before the Lord: How do I live the Eucharist? Do I live it anonymously or as a moment of true communion with the Lord, and also with all the brothers and sisters who share this same banquet?

— Homily, May 30, 2013

Reflection: Take some time to meditate on Pope Francis' questions.

The Very Flesh of Christ

We cannot become starched Christians, those over-educated Christians who speak of theological matters as they calmly sip their tea. No! We must become courageous Christians and go in search of the people who are the very flesh of Christ, those who are the flesh of Christ!

— Address, Vigil of Pentecost With the
Ecclesial Movements, May 18, 2013

Reflection: When have you behaved like a starched Christian? When have you avoided others or kept your distance from them? Make time this week to greet and talk with those you encounter.

Rampant Capitalism

We must recover the whole sense of gift, of gratuitousness, of solidarity. Rampant capitalism has taught the logic of profit at all costs, of giving to get, of exploitation without looking at the person ... and we see the results in the crisis we are experiencing!

— Address, May 21, 2013

Reflection: How can you love others this week without asking for anything in return?

Especially You and I

Every Christian, and especially you and I, is called to be a bearer of this message of hope that gives serenity and joy: God's consolation, his tenderness toward all. But if we first experience the joy of being consoled by him, of being loved by him, then we can bring that joy to others. This is important if our mission is to be fruitful: to feel God's consolation and to pass it on to others!

— Homily, June 29, 2013

Reflection: Have you felt the consolation of the Lord? Plan to go on a retreat to help you find or renew the joy of being loved by him.

A Flame That Grows Stronger

You have been able to enjoy the wonderful experience of meeting Jesus.... But the experience of this encounter must not remain locked up in your life or in the small group of your parish, your movement, or your community. That would be like withholding oxygen from a flame that was burning strongly. Faith is a flame that grows stronger the more it is shared and passed on, so that everyone may know, love, and confess Jesus Christ, the Lord of life and history.

— Homily, World Youth Day, Closing Mass, July 28, 2013

Reflection: Think about the times that you shared your faith with others. How did your faith grow in this process? Who can you share the faith with this week?

A New Song

The opening words of the psalm that we proclaimed are: "Sing to the LORD a new song" (Psalm 96:1). What is this new song? It does not consist of words, it is not a melody, it is the song of your life, it is allowing our life to be identified with that of Jesus, it is sharing his sentiments, his thoughts, his actions. And the life of Jesus is a life for others. The life of Jesus is a life for others. It is a life of service.

— Homily, World Youth Day, Closing Mass, July 28, 2013

Reflection: What is the song of your life? Do you need to change your tune?

His Voice Warms My Heart

However Jesus, at a certain point, said: "My Father, who has given them to me ..." (John 10:29), referring to his sheep. This is very important; it is a profound mystery, far from easy to understand. If I feel drawn to Jesus, if his voice warms my heart, it is thanks to God the Father who has sown within me the desire for love, for truth, for life, for beauty ... and Jesus is all this in fullness!

— *Regina Caeli* address, April 21, 2013

Reflection: Recall your journey with the Lord and the faith that he has sown within you. Take time to thank God for his grace. Ask him how you can use these gifts for his glory.

Living as a Gift

Jesus says something remarkable to us: "Greater love has no man than this, that a man lay down his life for his friends." Love always takes this path: to give one's life. To live life as a gift, a gift to be given — not a treasure to be stored away. And Jesus lived it in this manner, as a gift. And if we live life as a gift, we do what Jesus wanted: "I appointed you that you should go and bear fruit."

— Homily, Domus Sanctae Marthae, May 14, 2013

Reflection: How is God asking you to lay down your life for others today?

Is It Jesus or the Devil?

It is true that the devil, and St. Paul says so, very often comes dressed up as an angel of light. He likes to imitate the light of Jesus. He makes himself seem good and speaks to us like that, calmly, just as Jesus spoke after fasting in the wilderness: Work this miracle "if you are the Son of God, throw yourself down" from the temple! ... We should ask the Lord insistently for the wisdom of discernment in order to recognize when it is Jesus who gives us light and when it is the devil himself, disguised as an angel of light.

Many believe they live in light, but they are in darkness and are unaware of it! If we are meek in our inner light, we are gentle people; we hear the voice of Jesus in our heart and look fearlessly at the Cross in the light of Jesus.... We must always make the distinction: Where Jesus is, there is always humility, meekness, love, and the Cross.

— Homily, Domus Sanctae Marthae, September 3, 2013

Reflection: What decisions have you made lately? Where do you turn for help when making decisions? Examine your choices in light of Pope Francis' criteria of humility, meekness, love, and the Cross.

A Roped Guide

The Ascension of Jesus into heaven acquaints us with this deeply consoling reality on our journey: In Christ, true God and true man, our humanity was taken to God. Christ opened the path to us. He is like a roped guide climbing a mountain who, on reaching the summit, pulls us up to him and leads us to God. If we entrust our life to him, if we let ourselves be guided by him, we are certain to be in safe hands, in the hands of our Savior, of our Advocate.

— General Audience, April 17, 2013

Reflection: In what ways is Jesus calling you to follow his path and example? What difficulties have you encountered? What people can help you along the way?

People Who Have Been Raised From the Dead

Dear brothers and sisters, let us point out the Risen Christ to those who ask us to account for the hope that is in us (cf. 1 Peter 3:15). Let us point him out with the proclamation of the Word, but above all with our lives as people who have been raised. Let us show the joy of being children of God, the freedom that living in Christ gives us, which is true freedom, the freedom that saves us from the slavery of evil, of sin, and of death!

— General Audience, April 10, 2013

Reflection: Think of some specific times when Jesus freed you from evil and sin. How can you continue to enjoy that freedom in your life this week?

She Did Not Wait

FEAST OF THE VISITATION OF THE BLESSED VIRGIN MARY

Our Lady, as soon as she had heard the news that she was to be the Mother of Jesus and the announcement that her cousin Elizabeth was expecting a child — the Gospel says — she went to her in haste, she did not wait. She did not say: "But now I am with child, I must take care of my health. My cousin is bound to have friends who can care for her." ... And Our Lady is always like this. She is our Mother who always hurries to us whenever we are in need.

— Homily, May 26, 2013

Reflection: Pray to Mary when you are in need. Learn to trust in her intercession. She will run to your aid "in haste"!

Close to Each One of Us

Dear brothers and sisters, the Ascension does not point to Jesus' absence but tells us that he is alive in our midst in a new way. He is no longer in a specific place in the world as he was before the Ascension. He is now in the lordship of God, present in every space and time, close to each one of us. In our life, we are never alone: we have this Advocate who awaits us.

— General Audience, April 17, 2013

Reflection: What are some ways to remind yourself that Jesus is in your midst each day? How can the reminder of his presence change your attitude, your decisions, and your actions?

Sacred Heart of Jesus

The month of June is traditionally dedicated to the Sacred Heart of Jesus, the greatest human expression of divine love. In fact, last Friday we celebrated the Solemnity of the Sacred Heart of Jesus, and this feast sets the tone for the entire month. Popular piety highly values symbols, and the Heart of Jesus is the ultimate symbol of God's mercy. But it is not an imaginary symbol; it is a real symbol which represents the center, the source from which salvation flowed for all of humanity.

— Angelus address, June 9, 2013

Reflection: Meditate on the meaning of Jesus' Sacred Heart, a heart full of love and mercy. Ask God to transform your heart into his.

Seek a Lawyer

When someone is summoned by the judge or is involved in legal proceedings, the first thing he does is to seek a lawyer to defend him. We have One who always defends us, who defends us from the snares of the devil, who defends us from ourselves and from our sins!

— General Audience, April 17, 2013

Reflection: God is always there when you fall. Ask him for help and encounter him in the sacrament of Penance.

Don't Fall Ill

At this time of crisis, we cannot be concerned solely with ourselves, withdrawing into loneliness, discouragement, and a sense of powerlessness in the face of problems. Please do not withdraw into yourselves! This is a danger: we shut ourselves up in the parish, with our friends, within the movement, with the like-minded ... but do you know what happens? When the Church becomes closed, she becomes an ailing Church, she falls ill!

... The Church must step outside herself. To go where? To the outskirts of existence, whatever they may be, but she must step out.

— Address, Vigil of Pentecost With the
Ecclesial Movements, May 18, 2013

Reflection: How can you help our Church step outside herself? What does that mean in your everyday life? If you decide to move out of your comfort zone, can you approach others on the outskirts of existence without judging them?

A Little Mercy

A little mercy makes the world less cold and more just. We need to understand properly this mercy of God, this merciful Father who is so patient.

— Angelus address, March 17, 2013

Reflection: Reflect on how patient God has been with you. With whom do you need to be patient?

A Scandal Is News

There is another important point: encountering the poor. If we step outside ourselves, we find poverty. Today — it sickens the heart to say so — the discovery of a tramp who has died of the cold is not news. Today what counts as news is, maybe, a scandal. A scandal: Ah, that is news! Today, the thought that a great many children do not have food to eat is not news. This is serious; this is serious! We cannot put up with this! Yet that is how things are.

— Address, Vigil of Pentecost With the
Ecclesial Movements, May 18, 2013

Reflection: Where does responding to the needs of the poor fall in your priorities? How can you reprioritize what really matters? Ask God to help you overcome any fears you have about serving the needy.

Don't Be a Pharisee

He comes for us, when we recognize that we are sinners. But if we are like the Pharisee, before the altar, who said: I thank you Lord, that I am not like other men, and especially not like the one at the door, like that publican (cf. Luke 18:11-12), then we do not know the Lord's heart, and we will never have the joy of experiencing this mercy!

— Homily, March 17, 2013

Reflection: Let us not forget God's greatest gift: his mercy. Ask God to help you develop a deeper gratitude for his mercy and a reduction in your pride.

Walls

Let us ask ourselves today: Are we open to "God's surprises"? Or are we closed and fearful before the newness of the Holy Spirit? Do we have the courage to strike out along the new paths which God's newness sets before us, or do we resist, barricaded in transient structures which have lost their capacity for openness to what is new? We would do well to ask ourselves these questions all through the day.

— Homily, Mass With the Ecclesial Movements
on Pentecost Sunday, May 19, 2013

Reflection: Before Pentecost, the apostles locked themselves in the Upper Room. But when they received the Holy Spirit, they were compelled to go and spread the Gospel. What barriers keep you from hearing the Holy Spirit and sharing the good news?

Sails

The older theologians used to say that the soul is a kind of sailboat, the Holy Spirit is the wind which fills its sails and drives it forward, and the gusts of wind are the gifts of the Spirit. Lacking his impulse and his grace, we do not go forward.

— Homily, Mass With the Ecclesial Movements
on Pentecost Sunday, May 19, 2013

Reflection: Are your sails open? Which direction is your boat headed? Take some time to reorient your life and ask God for the grace to get you where he wants you to go.

Be Missionaries of God's Mercy

Each individual Christian and every community is missionary to the extent that they ... live the Gospel, and testify to God's love for all, especially those experiencing difficulties. Be missionaries of God's love and tenderness! Be missionaries of God's mercy, which always forgives us, always awaits us and loves us dearly.

— Homily, May 5, 2013

Reflection: Are you called to be a missionary to certain people in your everyday life? How can you love them so that they experience the Gospel as good news, meant for them?

Difficulties

It takes courage to begin following Jesus Christ. And this courage comes from God. When you're being abused and insulted, you need endurance in order to withstand all the difficulties of everyday life, all the difficulties of preaching the Gospel.

You need apostolic stamina to endure all the difficulties inflicted by those whom Paul himself describes as enemies of the Cross of Christ — those people who like to be flattered and who like to be told what they like to hear; those people who want to be told what they want the Gospel to say and not what the Gospel says. For this reason, Paul says: "We never used words of flattery" (see 1 Thessalonians 2:5).

— *Only Love Can Save Us*, Homily, August 4, 2006

Reflection: Have you heard the saying, "Don't tell God how big your storm is; tell the storm how big your God is"? The Lord — who is bigger than anything you face — will give you the courage and endurance to deal with your challenges and to preach the Gospel. Ask him for help, now and throughout the day.

Encounter

In this "stepping out," it is important to be ready for encounter. For me, this word is very important. Encounter with others. Why? Because faith is an encounter with Jesus, and we must do what Jesus does: encounter others ... we must create a "culture of encounter," a culture of friendship, a culture in which we find brothers and sisters, in which we can also speak with those who think differently, as well as those who hold other beliefs, who do not have the same faith.

— Address, Vigil of Pentecost With the
Ecclesial Movements, May 18, 2013

Reflection: How can you slow down to really encounter others and to learn more about their lives, their families, their activities, and their struggles? Find two times this week to truly encounter others.

Attractive and Persuasive

Christian truth is attractive and persuasive because it responds to the profound need of human life, proclaiming convincingly that Christ is the one Savior of the whole man and of all men. This proclamation remains as valid today as it was at the origin of Christianity.

— Address, March 15, 2013

Reflection: Are you convinced of the need that humans have for Jesus Christ? Don't underestimate how much people need Christ in their lives. We were all made for him.

Not a God "Spray"

Let us recognize that God is not something vague, our God is not a God "spray," he is tangible; he is not abstract but has a name: "God is love." His is not a sentimental, emotional kind of love but the love of the Father who is the origin of all life, the love of the Son who dies on the Cross and is raised, the love of the Spirit who renews human beings and the world.

— Angelus address, May 26, 2013

Reflection: Do you want God to be more real to you? Meet him in the Eucharist, where he is present to you, and meditate on the Cross, where he shows a definitive sign of love for you.

Walking With Us

The Most Holy Trinity is not the product of human reasoning but the face with which God actually revealed himself, not from the heights of a throne, but walking with humanity. It is Jesus himself who revealed the Father to us and who promised us the Holy Spirit.

God walked with his people in the history of the People of Israel, and Jesus has always walked with us and promised us the Holy Spirit, who is fire, who teaches us everything we do not know, and from within us guides us, gives us good ideas and good inspirations.

— Angelus address, May 26, 2013

Reflection: Our earthly fathers often walked with us through life. Our heavenly Father continues to walk with us here on earth. Take time to have a conversation with your heavenly Father. Ask him to guide and inspire you.

Soap Bubbles

The culture of comfort, which makes us think only of ourselves, makes us insensitive to the cries of other people, makes us live in soap bubbles which, however lovely, are insubstantial; they offer a fleeting and empty illusion which results in indifference to others; indeed, it even leads to the globalization of indifference. In this globalized world, we have fallen into globalized indifference.

— Homily, July 8, 2013

Reflection: What are some practical and specific ways you can be more sensitive to the needs of others around you? Make the decision now to begin to practice this new sensitivity no matter what the cost to your own comfort.

Left or Right?

Lastly, a word about the passage on the Last Judgment in which the Lord's Second Coming is described, when he will judge all human beings, the living and the dead (cf. Matthew 25:31-46). The image used by the Evangelist is that of the shepherd who separates the sheep from the goats. On his right, he places those who have acted in accordance with God's will, who went to the aid of their hungry, thirsty, foreign, naked, sick, or imprisoned neighbor.... While on his left are those who did not help their neighbor. This tells us that God will judge us on our love, on how we have loved our brethren, especially the weakest and the neediest.

— General Audience, April 24, 2013

Reflection: Imagine standing before God's throne at the end of your life. Would you be on his right or left side? Trust in God's mercy and grace to live a life dedicated to loving him and others.

Mortify Our Selfishness

This is a lesson for each one of us, but also for the Church of our time: if we let ourselves be led by the Holy Spirit, if we are able to mortify our selfishness to make room for the Lord's love and for his will, we will find peace, we will be builders of peace and will spread peace around us.

— Address, June 3, 2013

Reflection: How can you "mortify your selfishness"? Pick something to give up or do toward that goal this week.

Remote Controls

Jesus does not want selfish Christians who follow their own ego, who do not talk to God. Nor does he want weak Christians, Christians who have no will of their own, "remote-controlled" Christians incapable of creativity, who always seek to connect with the will of someone else and are not free. Jesus wants us free.

— Angelus address, June 30, 2013

Reflection: How can you strengthen your prayer life so that you rely more on God and less on the whims of your own ego? If you are sometimes a "remote-controlled" Christian, ask yourself why? What would happen if you allowed yourself to experience the creativity and freedom for which you were created?

What Is Magnanimity?

Magnanimity: This virtue of the great and the small.... What does being magnanimous mean? It means having a great heart, having greatness of mind; it means having great ideals, the wish to do great things to respond to what God asks of us.

Hence also, for this very reason, to do well the routine things of every day and all the daily actions, tasks, meetings with people; doing the little everyday things with a great heart open to God and to others. It is therefore important to cultivate human formation with a view to magnanimity.

— Address, To the Students of the Jesuit Schools
of Italy and Albania, June 6, 2013

Reflection: Most of us want to be great-hearted and filled with enthusiasm for life, but then reality sets in. If you're in a slump, ask God to help you find your way out. Start by practicing generosity of spirit in the smallest details of your routine today.

Must Be Free

In our daily prayers let us say to Jesus: "Lord, look at this brother, look at this sister who is suffering so much, suffering atrociously!" They experience the limit, the very limit between life and death. And there are consequences for us: this experience must spur us to promote religious freedom for everyone, everyone! Every man and every woman must be free in his or her profession of religion, whatever it may be. Why? Because that man and that woman are children of God.

— Address, Vigil of Pentecost With the
Ecclesial Movements, May 18, 2013

Reflection: In your daily prayers, pray for those who are not allowed to freely practice their faith. Pray for Christians who are persecuted around the world, and pray for people of all faiths.

Small Martyrs

FEAST OF STS. JOHN FISHER AND THOMAS MORE

To proclaim the Gospel, two virtues are essential: courage and patience [acceptance of suffering]. They [Christians who are suffering] are in the Church of "patience." They suffer, and there are more martyrs today than there were in the early centuries of the Church. More martyrs! Our own brothers and sisters. They are suffering! They carry their faith even to martyrdom. However, martyrdom is never a defeat; martyrdom is the highest degree of the witness we must give. We are on the way to martyrdom, as small martyrs: giving up this, doing that ... but we are on the way.

— Address, Vigil of Pentecost With the
Ecclesial Movements, May 18, 2013

Reflection: What can you learn from the martyrs, especially those of the twenty-first century? What small martyrdoms can you suffer in your daily life?

Waiting for You

We say we must seek God, go to him and ask forgiveness, but when we go, he is waiting for us, he is there first! In Spanish, we have a word that explains this well: *primerear* — the Lord always gets there before us, he gets there first, he is waiting for us!

— Address, Vigil of Pentecost With the
Ecclesial Movements, May 18, 2013

Reflection: We've all had situations where we know God is waiting for us to do something. He has gone ahead of us and prepared a path and a course of action. Does he want you to reach out to someone? Does he want you to spend more time in prayer? Where is God waiting for you?

Giving Your Life for the Truth

THE NATIVITY OF ST. JOHN THE BAPTIST

One of those who gave his life for the truth is John the Baptist ... June 24 is his great feast, the solemnity of his birth.... He died for the sake of the truth, when he denounced the adultery of King Herod and Herodias. How many people pay dearly for their commitment to truth! Upright people who are not afraid to go against the current! How many just men prefer to go against the current, so as not to deny the voice of conscience, the voice of truth! And we, we must not be afraid!

— Angelus address, June 23, 2013

Reflection: It is hard to stand up for the truth in our culture today. How can you stand up for truth in your decisions at work and in your family?

Listening to His Word

Another good way to grow in friendship with Christ is by listening to his word. The Lord speaks to us in the depths of our conscience, he speaks to us through Sacred Scripture, he speaks to us in prayer. Learn to stay before him in silence to read and meditate on the Bible, especially the Gospels, to converse with him every day in order to feel his presence of friendship and love.

— Message, June 21, 2013

Reflection: We always want to hear Jesus' voice as we move through life, and God has given us his word in the Bible so that we can hear from him there. One good place to begin is by reading through the Gospel of John. Use this Gospel as a starting point for conversing with him.

Not Chosen for Little Things

Commit yourselves to great ideals, to the most important things. We Christians were not chosen by the Lord for little things; push onward toward the highest principles.

— Homily, Holy Mass With the Rite of Confirmation,
April 28, 2013

Reflection: What principles do you live by? Where is God seeking to push you further?

A Church With Open Doors

Are we able to communicate the face of a Church which is "home" to all? We sometimes speak of a Church that has its doors closed, but here we are contemplating much more than a Church with open doors, much more! We must, together, build this "home," build this Church, make this "home." A Church with closed doors or open doors; the task is to move forward and help build the Church.

The challenge is to rediscover, through the means of social communication as well as by personal contact, the beauty that is at the heart of our existence and journey, the beauty of faith and of the beauty of the encounter with Christ.

— Address, September 21, 2013

Reflection: What does it mean to share the beauty and truth of the faith from a Church with open doors? How is God calling you to make your local parish more like a home?

Slumbering Christians

What he asks of us is to be ready for the encounter — ready for an encounter, for a beautiful encounter, the encounter with Jesus, which means being able to see the signs of his presence, keeping our faith alive with prayer, with the sacraments, and taking care not to fall asleep so as to not forget about God. The life of slumbering Christians is a sad life; it is not a happy life. Christians must be happy, with the joy of Jesus. Let us not fall asleep!

— General Audience, April 24, 2013

Reflection: In what area of your faith life have you fallen asleep? How can you be more attentive to what God is trying to show you?

Two Glorious Witnesses

Feast of Sts. Peter and Paul

Dear brothers and sisters, what a joy to believe in a God who is all love, all grace! This is the faith that Peter and Paul received from Christ and passed on to the Church. Let us praise the Lord for these two glorious witnesses, and like them let us allow ourselves to be won over by Christ, by the mercy of Christ.

— Angelus address, June 23, 2013

Reflection: Sts. Peter and Paul both turned their back on our Lord. Peter denied Jesus three times, and Paul imprisoned and murdered Christians. Yet, each encountered the Lord's mercy, asked for forgiveness, and followed after our Lord. Whose life do you identify with more, St. Peter or St. Paul? How is God calling you to follow after them as they have followed Jesus?

Rigid Christians

Rigid Christians think that to be Christian it is necessary to wear mourning [and always] to take everything seriously.... They are very numerous. They are not Christians. They disguise themselves as Christians. [They] do not know Jesus, do not know who the Lord is, do not know what the rock is, they have none of the freedom of Christians.... In their life, there is no room for the Holy Spirit.

— Homily, Domus Sanctae Marthae, June 27, 2013

Reflection: Do you lack joy? Do you lack freedom? Are you are a rigid Christian? Put on the Holy Spirit and you will find yourself opening up to new opportunities. Not relying on ourselves gives us freedom. Trusting in the Lord gives us joy.

You Are Not Christians

All of us have enemies — all of us. Some are weak enemies, some strong. So often we, too, become the enemies of others; we do not love them. Jesus tells us that we must love our enemies.... We think that Jesus is asking too much of us. We think: "Let's leave this to the cloistered sisters who are holy, a few holy souls!" [But] Jesus says that you must do this, otherwise you are like the publicans, like the pagans, and you are not Christians....

— Homily, Domus Sanctae Marthae, June 18, 2013

Reflection: Who are your enemies? Do you pray for them? Do you forgive them? Do you love them?

Lowered Himself

Jesus Christ did not save us with an idea, or an intellectual program. He saved us with his flesh, with the concreteness of the flesh. He lowered himself, became man, and was made flesh until the end.

— Homily, Domus Sanctae Marthae, June 14, 2013

Reflection: Christianity as an intellectual program with no demands would be easier than following the narrow path of faith. How can you live out Jesus' model of humility by humbling yourself for the sake of others?

Does Not Believe

FEAST OF ST. THOMAS THE APOSTLE

Thomas does not believe it when the other apostles tell him: "We have seen the Lord." It isn't enough for him that Jesus had foretold it, promised it: "On the third day I will rise." He wants to see, he wants to put his hand in the place of the nails and in Jesus' side. And how does Jesus react? With patience: Jesus does not abandon Thomas in his stubborn unbelief; he gives him a week's time, he does not close the door, he waits.

— Homily, Divine Mercy Sunday, April 7, 2013

Reflection: How are you like Thomas sometimes? How do you think the Lord reacts to you?

The True Meaning of Freedom

INDEPENDENCE DAY

But what does freedom mean? It is certainly not doing whatever you want, allowing yourself to be dominated by the passions, to pass from one experience to another without discernment, to follow the fashions of the day; freedom does not mean, so to speak, throwing everything that you don't like out the window. No, that is not freedom! Freedom is given to us so that we know how to make good decisions in life!

— Address, May 4, 2013

Reflection: Freedom isn't freedom *from* something, but freedom *for* something. Are you free to choose what is good for your life? Are you free to live a life for the Lord instead of yourself? What limits your freedom?

No, This Money Is Mine

But when I had to come to Rome ... I often visited the Church of St. Louis of France, and I went there to contemplate the painting of "The Calling of St. Matthew," by Caravaggio.... That finger of Jesus, pointing at Matthew. That's me. I feel like him. Like Matthew.... It is the gesture of Matthew that strikes me: he holds on to his money as if to say, "No, not me! No, this money is mine." Here, this is me, a sinner on whom the Lord has turned his gaze. And this is what I said when they asked me if I would accept my election as pontiff.... I am a sinner, but I trust in the infinite mercy and patience of our Lord Jesus Christ, and I accept in a spirit of penance.

— Interview With Pope Francis, *America* magazine,
September 30, 2013

Reflection: What has Christ called you to do? Does the experience of being a sinner help you to bring humility and reliance on the Lord to this task?

A Slave to All

In our Second Reading today, St. Paul says: "I have made myself a slave to all, that I might win the more" (1 Corinthians 9:19). In order to proclaim Jesus, Paul made himself "a slave to all." Evangelizing means bearing personal witness to the love of God; it is overcoming our selfishness; it is serving by bending down to wash the feet of our brethren, as Jesus did.

— Homily, World Youth Day, Closing Mass, July 28, 2013

Reflection: What does it mean, specifically, for you to make yourself "a slave" to others in order to win them over to Jesus? How is God asking you to be selfless in reaching out to others?

We Know Something Is Missing

In the midst of ... a very aggressive pagan culture ... our hearts shrink back because we feel powerless. We adopt a minimalist attitude just trying to survive as we attempt to preserve our faith. However, we are not stupid; we know something is missing.... Could it be that we try to do everything by ourselves, thus losing our focus and feeling responsible for coming up with all the solutions? We know that we cannot do it alone.

Here is the question: Do we give time and space to our Lord during the day so he can do his work, or are we so busy doing everything by ourselves that we do not let him enter?

— *Only Love Can Save Us*, Letter to Priests and Religious, July 29, 2007

Reflection: Take some time to meditate on the Holy Father's questions.

Careerism

When a priest takes the road of vanity, he enters into the spirit of careerism and does great damage to the Church.... He boasts; he likes to be seen as high and mighty. And the people don't like it! You see what our difficulties and our temptations are; so you should pray for us that we be humble, gentle, and at the service of the people.

— Homily, Domus Sanctae Marthae, May 15, 2013

Reflection: Pray for your priests, deacons, religious, and seminarians this week by fasting from something you enjoy.

Go Out

But I want you to make yourselves heard in your dioceses, I want the noise to go out, I want the Church to go out onto the streets, I want us to resist everything worldly, everything static, everything comfortable, everything to do with clericalism, everything that might make us closed in on ourselves. The parishes, the schools, the institutions, are made for going out.

— Address, World Youth Day, July 25, 2013

Reflection: Are you making noise? What are you doing to resist what's comfortable in your life? What steps are you taking to keep from being closed in on yourself?

Sin Makes the Headlines

In the media, holiness is not news; outrage and sin make the headlines. How can this be a fair fight? Who can fight against this? Do some of us possibly dream we can fight with merely human means...? Be careful.... Our struggle is not against human powers but against the powers of darkness (see Ephesians 6:12). Just as it happened to Jesus (see Matthew 4:1-11), Satan is seeking to seduce us, to disorient us, to offer us "viable alternatives".... We need to find refuge in the power of the Word of God like Jesus did in the desert.

We need to resort to begging in prayer: ... the prayer of the humble and poor without any resources. The humble have nothing to lose. In fact, God reveals the way to them (see Matthew 11:25-26).... We cannot simply relax in our complacency.... This is the time for prayer.

— *Only Love Can Save Us*, Letter to Priests and Religious, July 29, 2007

Reflection: Do you really believe that Satan is seeking to seduce and disorient you? If this is the case, how are you fighting this battle? Pray for the strength to resist temptation, and spread God's love to others.

As Christ Understood It

The Holy Spirit teaches us to see with the eyes of Christ, to live life as Christ lived, to understand life as Christ understood it. That is why the living water, who is the Holy Spirit, quenches our life, why he tells us that we are loved by God as children, that we can love God as his children, and that by his grace we can live as children of God, like Jesus.

— General Audience, May 8, 2013

Reflection: As Jesus looks at your life, how do you think he views your struggles and hopes? He wants you to see with his eyes, so ask him to guide you as you strengthen the good, correct the weak, and work to conform your life to the Gospel.

Not in the Abstract

God sets beside us people who help us on our journey of faith. We do not find our faith in the abstract, no! It is always a person preaching who tells us who Jesus is, who communicates faith to us and gives us the first proclamation.

— Address, Vigil of Pentecost With the
Ecclesial Movements, May 18, 2013

Reflection: Which people encourage you in your efforts to go deeper in your walk with God? Find time to be with them this month.

Dump-Truck Culture

How easily do consciences become numb when there is no love! This numbness is indicative of a narcosis of the spirit and of life. We deliver our lives and, much worse, the lives of our children and our young people to such magical and destructive solutions as drugs ... gambling, trivial entertainment, and an inordinate concern for our bodies bordering on a fetish, all of which are entrenched in our narcissism and our consumer mentality.

And as for the elderly among us, who are merely disposable items according to this narcissistic consumer mentality, we simply throw them into an existential dump truck. As a result, this lack of love creates a "dump-truck culture." If it doesn't work, it's thrown away.

— *Only Love Can Save Us*, Homily, May 25, 2012

Reflection: Where there is disregard and selfishness, how can you sow dignity and love?

Insult First, Talk Later

What we usually hear nowadays — you only need to turn on the radio or watch television to hear it — is condemn first and talk after. Insult first; we'll talk about it afterward. An attitude that says, "He who hits first, hits twice." But this is not the logic of love.... Establishing love is a work of skillful craftsmanship, the work of patient people, people who do their utmost to persuade, to listen, to bring people together.

— *Only Love Can Save Us*, Homily, September 6, 2008

Reflection: It's easy to judge others. How can we build habits of patience and forgiveness? Who in your life needs this "logic of love" the most right now?

New Roads

Techniques of evangelization are important, of course, but even the most perfect ones could not replace the gentle action of the One who is the principal agent of evangelization: the Holy Spirit (cf. *Evangelii Nuntiandi*, n. 75). We must let ourselves be guided by him, even if he leads us on new roads; we must allow him to transform us, so that in our proclamation, our words are always accompanied by a simple life, a spirit of prayer, charity to all, especially the lowly and the poor, humility and detachment from ourselves, and holiness of life (cf. ibid., n. 76).

— Address, June 13, 2013

Reflection: Where is God looking to transform your life? Is he calling you to travel on new roads? Are you willing to hear that call?

No Borders, No Limits

Where does Jesus send us? There are no borders, no limits: he sends us to everyone. The Gospel is for everyone, not just for some. It is not only for those who seem closer to us, more receptive, more welcoming. It is for everyone.

Do not be afraid to go and to bring Christ into every area of life, to the fringes of society, even to those who seem farthest away, most indifferent. The Lord seeks all; he wants everyone to feel the warmth of his mercy and his love.

— Homily, World Youth Day, Closing Mass, July 28, 2013

Reflection: What does a church look like when it is intent on sharing the Good News with everyone? Can you help your parish look like that?

Loved Us, Saved Us, Forgiven Us

The apostle Paul ended this passage of his letter to our forebears with these words: You are no longer under law but under grace [see Romans 6:14]. And this is our life: walking under grace, because the Lord has loved us, has saved us, has forgiven us. The Lord has done all things and this is grace, God's grace. We are on our way under the grace of God, who came down to us in Jesus Christ who saved us.

— Address, June 17, 2013

Reflection: God's grace covers our journey with God from beginning to end. Thank God for loving you first, and ask for an open heart to accept his grace more deeply in your life.

How to Proclaim the Gospel Without Soul

A new evangelization, a Church which evangelizes, must always start with prayer, with asking, like the apostles in the Upper Room, for the fire of the Holy Spirit. Only a faithful and intense relationship with God makes it possible to get out of our own closedness and proclaim the Gospel with *parrhesia* [courage]. Without prayer, our acts are empty, and our proclamation has no soul; it is not inspired by the Spirit.

— General Audience, May 22, 2013

Reflection: Do you make prayer a priority each day? How healthy would it be for a married couple to go for days without speaking to each other? Enkindle your relationship with God each day through meaningful time in prayer.

Builders of Their Own Destiny

Listen! Young people are the window through which the future enters the world. They are the window, and so they present us with great challenges. Our generation will show that it can rise to the promise found in each young person when we know how to give them space.

This means that we have to create the material and spiritual conditions for their full development; to give them a solid basis on which to build their lives; to guarantee their safety and their education to be everything they can be; to pass on to them lasting values that make life worth living; to give them a transcendent horizon for their thirst for authentic happiness and their creativity for the good; to give them the legacy of a world worthy of human life; and to awaken in them their greatest potential as builders of their own destiny, sharing responsibility for the future of everyone.

— Address, July 22, 2013

Reflection: What can you do to help young people find their potential? What gifts or skills can you share with them? Are there opportunities in your parish or local schools to connect with and encourage them?

Rebuild My House

I think of the story of St. Francis of Assisi. In front of the crucifix, he heard the voice of Jesus saying to him: "Francis, go, rebuild my house." The young Francis responded readily and generously to the Lord's call to rebuild his house. But which house? Slowly but surely, Francis came to realize that it was not a question of repairing a stone building, but about doing his part for the life of the Church. It was a matter of being at the service of the Church, loving her, and working to make the countenance of Christ shine ever more brightly in her.

— Address, Prayer Vigil, July 27, 2013

Reflection: It took St. Francis of Assisi many years to finally understand and surrender to God's call in his life. If you're unsure what you should do or where you should go, and you're waiting for some direction from the Lord, serve him generously where you are as you wait for his plan to unfold.

A Sower

We all know the parable where Jesus speaks of a sower who went out to sow seeds in the field; some seed fell on the path, some on rocky ground, some among thorns, and could not grow; other seed fell on good soil and brought forth much fruit (cf. Matthew 13:1-9). Jesus himself explains the meaning of the parable: the seed is the Word of God sown in our hearts (cf. Matthew 13:18-23).

Today ... every day, but today in a particular way, Jesus is sowing the seed. When we accept the Word of God, then we are the Field of Faith! Please, let Christ and his word enter your life; let the seed of the Word of God enter, let it blossom, and let it grow.

— Address, World Youth Day, July 27, 2013

Reflection: What kind of soil are you? Where do you have rocky ground or thorns? Where do you need the Word of God to enter your life?

Look Upon the Stones, Thorns, and Weeds

I know that you want to be good soil, true Christians, authentic Christians, not part-time Christians: "starchy," aloof, and Christian in "appearance only." I know that you don't want to be duped by a false freedom, always at the beck and call of momentary fashions and fads. I know that you are aiming high, at long-lasting decisions which are meaningful....

Let's do this: in silence ... say to him: Jesus, look upon the stones, the thorns, and the weeds that I have, but look also upon this small piece of ground that I offer to you so that the seed may enter my heart. In silence, let us allow the seed of Jesus to enter our hearts.

— Address, World Youth Day, Prayer Vigil, July 27, 2013

Reflection: Think over Pope Francis' words, and in silence pray as Pope Francis recommends, asking the seed of Jesus to enter your heart.

The Church as a Body

The Church is not a welfare, cultural, or political association but a living body that walks and acts in history. And this body has a head, Jesus, who guides, feeds, and supports it. This is a point that I would like to emphasize: If one separates the head from the rest of the body, the whole person cannot survive. It is like this in the Church: we must stay ever more deeply connected with Jesus.

But not only that: just as it is important that life blood flow through the body in order to live, so must we allow Jesus to work in us, let his Word guide us, his presence in the Eucharist feed us, give us life, his love strengthen our love for our neighbor. And this forever! Forever and ever!

— General Audience, June 19, 2013

Reflection: Are you connected to the Church? Are you united to the Body of Christ? Find time this week to go to daily Mass and get even more connected.

Mercy: A Proper Remedy

Love neither discriminates nor relativizes because it is merciful. And mercy creates even greater closeness ... and, since it truly wishes to help, it seeks the truth that hurts the most — that of sin — but with the aim of finding its proper remedy.

This love is both personal and communitarian. It ... sets a slower pace (helping those who are sick takes time) and creates welcoming and inclusive structures — a process that also requires time.

— *Only Love Can Save Us*, First Regional Congress of Urban Ministry in Buenos Aires, August 25, 2011

Reflection: Why do we so easily judge others? We quickly categorize people and decide whether or not we will interact with them. Where is God calling you to be more welcoming? Where have you failed in this regard?

Witness to the Gospel

We all have to proclaim and bear witness to the Gospel. We should all ask ourselves: How do I bear witness to Christ through my faith? Do I have the courage of Peter and the other apostles, to think, to choose, and to live as a Christian, obedient to God?

— Homily, April 14, 2013

Reflection: Spend a few minutes reflecting on Pope Francis' question: How do you bear witness to Christ through your faith?

Are You There for Them?

FEAST OF STS. JOACHIM AND ANNE

Mary continues to accompany life. Do I, like Mary, remain steadfast? How are your parents? How are your grandparents? How are your in-laws? Are you there for them? Do you care about them? Do you visit them? Sometimes it is very painful, but there is no other choice than to put them in a nursing home for health reasons or family situations. But once they are there, do I set aside a Saturday or a Sunday to be with them? Do you care about that life that is fading away and that gave life to you?

— *Only Love Can Save Us*, Homily, Feast of the Annunciation, March 25, 2011

Reflection: Do you set aside time to be with your family members? If they live far away, do you make it a priority to call or e-mail to send them little reminders of your love for them?

Theological Brainwashing

Today there exists a great temptation in the Church which is a spiritual form of "abuse": to manipulate the mind; a sort of theological brainwashing which ultimately brings one to a superficial meeting with Christ but not to an encounter with the Person of Christ Alive! Within this encounter, there is the person and there is Christ. There is no room for the spiritual engineer who wishes to manipulate.

This is the challenge: to bring the person to Christ. This must be done, however, in complete awareness that we ourselves are means of communication and that the real problem does not concern the acquisition of the latest technologies, even if these make a valid presence possible. It is necessary to be absolutely clear that the God in whom we believe, who loves all men and women intensely, wants to reveal himself through the means at our disposal, however poor they are, because it is he who is at work, he who transforms and saves us.

— Address, September 21, 2013

Reflection: How do you have true and meaningful encounters with our Lord that are not superficial? Speak to the Lord about your hopes, your weaknesses, your failures, and your fears. Bring the fruit of this encounter with the person of Christ into your conversations with others.

In Material Things or Jesus?

Today, it would be good for all of us to ask ourselves sincerely: In whom do we place our trust? In ourselves, in material things, or in Jesus? We all have the temptation often to put ourselves at the center, to believe that we are the axis of the universe, to believe that we alone build our lives or to think that our life can only be happy if built on possessions, money, or power. But we all know that it is not so.

Certainly, possessions, money, and power can give a momentary thrill, the illusion of being happy, but they end up possessing us and making us always want to have more, never satisfied. And we end up "full," but not nourished, and it is very sad to see young people "full," but weak. Young people must be strong, nourished by the faith and not filled with other things! "Put on Christ" in your life, place your trust in him and you will never be disappointed!

— Address, World Youth Day, July 25, 2013

Reflection: What fills you up? What desires do you have that ought to be fulfilled by God instead of something else? Take time in the quiet of your heart to place your trust in God and him alone.

A Worldly Spirit

However, there is one problem that can afflict Christians: the spirit of the world, the worldly spirit, spiritual worldliness. This leads to self-sufficiency, to living by the spirit of the world rather than by the spirit of Jesus.

— Address, Vigil of Pentecost With the
Ecclesial Movements, May 18, 2013

Reflection: Think about where you can replace the spirit of the world with the spirit of Jesus. In your friendships? In the media you consume? In your attitude? Make a concrete effort to live by his spirit this week.

Behave as True Children

Yet this filial relationship with God is not like a treasure that we keep in a corner of our life.... It must be nourished every day with listening to the Word of God, with prayer, with participation in the sacraments, especially Reconciliation and the Eucharist, and with love.

We can live as children! And this is our dignity — we have the dignity of children. We should behave as true children! This means that every day we must let Christ transform us and conform us to him; it means striving to live as Christians, endeavoring to follow him in spite of seeing our limitations and weaknesses.

— General Audience, April 10, 2013

Reflection: Increase your faith by nourishing it. In what area are you weak? Find a way to correct and strengthen that area each day this month.

Difficult Moments

FEAST OF ST. IGNATIUS OF LOYOLA

[On the difficulty of making the decision to become a priest and a Jesuit]: You know, it is always difficult. Always. It was hard for me. It is far from easy. There are beautiful moments, and Jesus helps you, he gives you a little joy. All the same there are difficult moments when you feel alone, when you feel dry, without any interior joy. There are clouded moments of interior darkness. There are hardships.

But it is so beautiful to follow Jesus, to walk in the footsteps of Jesus, that you then find balance and move forward. And then come even more wonderful moments. But no one must think that there will not be difficult moments in life.

— Address, To the Students of the Jesuit Schools of Italy and Albania, June 6, 2013

Reflection: Think back to all of the major decisions you have made with the Lord. Where have there been hardships? What has been beautiful? Thank God for the past, and remember these moments as you walk with Jesus in the future.

Contagious Joy

Do not be afraid to show the joy of having answered the Lord's call, of having responded to his choice of love, and of bearing witness to his Gospel in service to the Church. And joy, true joy, is contagious; it is infectious ... it impels one forward.

— Address, To Seminarians and Novices, July 6, 2013

Reflection: Whom do you know who has this spirit of infectious joy? Can you speak with them and ask how they've grown in this? How can *you* grow in the Lord's joy?

Be Committed

And then I would like to speak especially to you young people: be committed to your daily duties, your studies, your work, to relationships of friendship, to helping others; your future also depends on how you live these precious years of your life. Do not be afraid of commitment, of sacrifice, and do not view the future with fear. Keep your hope alive: there is always a light on the horizon.

— General Audience, May 1, 2013

Reflection: What commitments are you afraid of? What step can you take today toward taking responsibility?

The Wine of Joy

God always surprises us, like the new wine in the Gospel we have just heard. God always saves the best for us. But he asks us to let ourselves be surprised by his love, to accept his surprises. Let us trust God! Cut off from him, the wine of joy, the wine of hope, runs out. If we draw near to him, if we stay with him, what seems to be cold water, difficulty, sin, is changed into the new wine of friendship with him.

— Homily, World Youth Day, July 24, 2013

Reflection: Read about the wedding feast at Cana in the Gospel of John (2:1-11) and meditate on it in prayer, together with the Holy Father's words above. What is God saying to you?

Peace Is a Precious Gift

Today, dear brothers and sisters, I wish to add my voice to the cry which rises up with increasing anguish from every part of the world, from every people, from the heart of each person, from the one great family which is humanity: it is the cry for peace! It is a cry which declares with force: We want a peaceful world, we want to be men and women of peace, and we want in our society, torn apart by divisions and conflict, that peace break out!

War never again! Never again war! Peace is a precious gift, which must be promoted and protected.

— Angelus address, September 1, 2013

Reflection: Examine your own life. Are you a person of peace? Do you look for opportunities for dialogue when you disagree with someone? How can you promote peace in your family, in your community, in the world?

Do You Want to Be My Disciple?

Looking out to this sea, the beach and all of you gathered here, I am reminded of the moment when Jesus called the first disciples to follow him by the shores of Lake Tiberias. Today Christ asks each of us again: Do you want to be my disciple? Do you want to be my friend? Do you want to be a witness to my Gospel?

— Address, World Youth Day, July 25, 2013

Reflection: Consider the pope's three questions above. How have you answered these questions in the past? How would you like to live them out in the future?

The Holy Spirit Annoys Us

FEAST OF THE TRANSFIGURATION OF THE LORD

The Holy Spirit annoys us, because he moves us, he makes us travel, he pushes the Church forward. And we are like Peter at the Transfiguration: "Oh, how wonderful it is for us to be here, all together!" as long as it does not inconvenience us.

We would like the Holy Spirit to doze off. We want to subdue the Holy Spirit. And that just will not work. For he is God, and he is that wind that comes and goes, and you do not know from where. He is the strength of God; it is he who gives us consolation and strength to continue forward. To go forward! And this is bothersome. Convenience is nicer.

— Homily, Domus Sanctae Marthae, April 16, 2013

Reflection: What inconvenient thing is the Holy Spirit asking you to do? How do you try to subdue what he tells you? How can you respond in greater freedom?

Real Meaning and Fulfillment

When we prepare a plate of food and we see that it needs salt, well, we "put on" salt; when it needs oil, then you "put on" oil. "To put on" — that is, to place on top of, to pour over. And so it is in our life.... If we want it to have real meaning and fulfillment, as you want and as you deserve, I say to each one of you, "Put on faith," and life will take on a new flavor, life will have a compass to show you the way; "put on hope," and every one of your days will be enlightened and your horizon will no longer be dark, but luminous; "put on love," and your life will be like a house built on rock, your journey will be joyful, because you will find many friends to journey with you.

— Address, World Youth Day, July 25, 2013

Reflection: The pope mentioned faith, hope, and love. Which of these virtues do you need the most right now? Which one do you need to "put on" today?

What Is Your Mentality?

We must have the courage of faith not to allow ourselves to be guided by the mentality that tells us: "God is not necessary, he is not important for you," and so forth. It is exactly the opposite: only by behaving as children of God, without despairing at our shortcomings, at our sins, only by feeling loved by him will our life be new, enlivened by serenity and joy. God is our strength! God is our hope!

— General Audience, April 10, 2013

Reflection: Our culture often tells us that God is not necessary or important. How can you remind yourself on a daily basis about the importance of God in your life?

A Criterion for Evaluation

So how does the Holy Spirit act in our life and in the life of the Church in order to guide us to the truth? First of all, he recalls and impresses in the heart of believers the words Jesus spoke and, through these very words, the law of God — as the prophets of the Old Testament had foretold — is engraved in our heart and becomes within us a criterion for evaluation in decisions and for guidance in our daily actions; it becomes a principle to live by.

— General Audience, May 15, 2013

Reflection: Do you have a decision to make, or are you wondering about a teaching of the Catholic Church? Take a look at the *Catechism of the Catholic Church* regarding the issue you are facing. If you don't own a copy, you can find it online. Trust the wisdom of the Church.

What Is the Most Important Thing?

What is the most important thing? Jesus. If we forge ahead with our own arrangements, with other things, with beautiful things but without Jesus, we make no headway, it does not work. Jesus is more important.

— Address, Vigil of Pentecost With the Ecclesial Movements, May 18, 2013

Reflection: What is the most important thing for you? Make Jesus the center of your decisions, activities, and words today in a specific and deliberate way.

Numbing Ourselves to Reality

Love today invites us to look beyond the short-term, taking a concern for the generations to come and not leaving them a legacy of easy solutions.... It invites us to move forward without numbing ourselves to reality, without being like ostriches burying their heads in the sand in face of failures and mistakes.

Love invites us to accept that in our very weakness is all the potential needed to reconstruct our lives, to be reconciled with each other, and to grow.

— *Only Love Can Save Us*, Homily, May 25, 2012

Reflection: What failures and mistakes do you need to face? Where is God asking you to grow?

The Main Character

At some point, we feel Jesus is looking at us. He always makes us feel as though he knows we are here, and he promises a deeper encounter in which we will be the main character in our friendship with him.

— *Only Love Can Save Us*, Homily, August 7, 2011

Reflection: In the story of life, do you consider yourself a main character? Do you play a starring role? If you consider yourself the main character, how does this perspective change your life?

Cultural Euthanasia

Look, at this moment, I think our world civilization has gone beyond its limits; it has gone beyond its limits because it has made money into such a god that we are now faced with a philosophy and a practice which exclude the two ends of life that are most full of promise for peoples. They exclude the elderly, obviously. You could easily think there is a kind of hidden euthanasia — that is, we don't take care of the elderly; but there is also a cultural euthanasia, because we don't allow them to speak, we don't allow them to act.

And there is the exclusion of the young. The percentage of our young people without work, without employment, is very high, and we have a generation with no experience of the dignity gained through work.

— Address, World Youth Day, July 25, 2013

Reflection: In a culture that seems to only be for itself, many people and priorities are left behind. What can you do this week to practice greater selflessness? What specific activity can you add to your schedule to help you achieve that goal?

Obsessed With the Culture of Encounter

Be servants of communion and of the culture of encounter! I would like you to be almost obsessed about this. Be so without being presumptuous, imposing "our truths," but rather be guided by the humble yet joyful certainty of those who have been found, touched, and transformed by the Truth who is Christ, ever to be proclaimed.

— Homily, World Youth Day, July 27, 2013

Reflection: Today, give your full attention to those you are speaking with. Have the humility to perform the loving act of listening.

Never Gloomy

FEAST OF THE ASSUMPTION OF THE BLESSED VIRGIN MARY

Christians are joyful; they are never gloomy. God is at our side. We have a Mother who always intercedes for the life of her children, for us, as Queen Esther did in the first reading (cf. Esther 5:3). Jesus has shown us that the face of God is that of a loving Father. Sin and death have been defeated. Christians cannot be pessimists!

— Homily, World Youth Day, July 24, 2013

Reflection: Do you struggle with pessimism? Read the life of a saint. Ask God to help you see and live out his or her perspective.

God Never Condemns

Let us remember this: God judges us by loving us. If I embrace his love, then I am saved; if I refuse it, then I am condemned, not by him, but my own self, because God never condemns; he only loves and saves.

— Address, World Youth Day, Way of the Cross, July 26, 2013

Reflection: When do you refuse God's love? Why?

Jesus Is Not an Illusion!

And when I say this, I want to be sincere and to tell you that I do not come here to sell you an illusion. I come here to say: There is a Person who can keep you going, trust in him! It is Jesus! Trust in Jesus! And Jesus is not an illusion! Trust in Jesus. The Lord is always with us. He comes to the shores of the sea of our life; he makes himself close to our failures, our frailty, and our sins in order to transform them. Never stop staking yourselves on him, over and over again, as good sportsmen — some of you know this well from experience — who can face the strain of training in order to achieve results!

Difficulties must not frighten you but on the contrary spur you to go beyond them. Hear Jesus' words as though they were addressed to you: Put out into the deep and let down your nets.

— Address, Meeting With Young People, September 22, 2013

Reflection: What difficulties are you facing right now? Do they frighten you? Take some time in the quiet of your heart to commit your life and your difficulties to Jesus. Ask God to make these difficulties an opportunity to trust in him and to grow stronger.

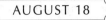

Do I?

So let us ask ourselves this evening, in adoring Christ, who is really present in the Eucharist: Do I let myself be transformed by him? Do I let the Lord, who gives himself to me, guide me to going out ever more from my little enclosure, in order to give, to share, to love him and others?

— Homily, May 30, 2013

Reflection: Meditate on the questions that Pope Francis asks, above.

Suicide of Humanity

War is madness. It is the suicide of humanity. It is an act of faith in money, which for the mighty of this earth is more important than people.... Today we ... pray for the dead, the wounded, for those victims of the madness that is war: the suicide of humanity — it kills the heart, it kills precisely the message of the Lord, it kills love.... God our Father weeps, weeps over this madness, and says to all who have power: Where is your brother? ... What have you done? ... O Lord, have mercy on us ... and forgive everyone of their sins.

Because behind a war, there are always sins: the sin of idolatry, exploiting people, sacrificing them on the altar of power. Turn to us, Lord. We are confident that the Lord will hear us. That he will do anything to give us the spirit of consolation.

— Homily, Domus Sanctae Marthae, June 2, 2013

Reflection: Our age is one filled with wars. Wars within various nations. Wars with our culture. Wars in our own hearts. What do you think God wants you to learn from all of this? How is he calling you to love others despite the madness that surrounds these wars?

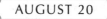

Do Not Lose Trust

You young people, my dear young friends, you have a particular sensitivity toward injustice, but you are often disappointed by facts that speak of corruption on the part of people who put their own interests before the common good. To you and to all, I repeat: Never yield to discouragement, do not lose trust, do not allow your hope to be extinguished.

Situations can change; people can change. Be the first to seek to bring good; do not grow accustomed to evil, but defeat it with good.

— Address, World Youth Day, July 25, 2013

Reflection: How can you bring a positive attitude to a discouraging situation? Consider the steps you might take to defeat evil with good. What action is needed for the situation? What patience is required?

Walk With God's People

Say no to hypocrisy. Say no to hypocritical clericalism. Say no to spiritual worldliness. If you don't, you're acting more like a businessman or an entrepreneur rather than a man or woman of the Gospel.

Say yes to closeness, to walking with God's people. Say yes to tenderness, especially toward sinners and toward outcasts, knowing that God dwells among them.

— *Only Love Can Save Us*, Homily, September 2, 2012

Reflection: When you are tempted today to react harshly to a situation, pause and consider how you might instead say "yes" to tenderness? Be a man or woman of the Gospel, a man or woman of mercy.

Nothing Slow About the Holy Spirit

In prayer, before God who speaks, in thinking and meditating on the facts of her life, Mary is not in a hurry, she does not let herself be swept away by the moment, she does not let herself be dragged along by events.

However, when she has clearly understood what God is asking of her, what she has to do, she does not loiter, she does not delay, but goes "with haste." St Ambrose commented: "There is nothing slow about the Holy Spirit" (*Expos. Evang. sec. Lucam*, II, 19: PL 15,1560).

— Address, May 31, 2013

Reflection: What events sweep you away from thinking about what's important in life? What keeps you from going with haste to do what God asks of you? Take time in prayer to listen to your Father, to hear his voice, and to respond to him.

Act of Justice

Each time a woman gives birth to a child, it is yet another bet placed for life and for the future; that, when we show concern for the innocence of children, we guarantee the truth of tomorrow; and that, when we esteem an unselfish elderly person, we are performing an act of justice and embracing our own roots.

— *Only Love Can Save Us*, Letter to the Priests, Religious, and Faithful of Buenos Aires, October 1, 2012

Reflection: Do you look for opportunities to care for the young and the elderly? Can you help a single mother in your parish or neighborhood? Visit a lonely elderly person in a nursing home? If you are a parent, think about bringing your children with you to model acts of service for them.

A Presence That Listens

We must ask ourselves: What role should the Church have in terms of the practical means of communication at her disposal? In every situation, beyond technological considerations, I believe that the goal is to understand how to enter into dialogue with the men and women of today.... They are men and women who sometimes feel let down by a Christianity that to them appears sterile and in difficulty as it tries to communicate the depth of meaning that comes with the gift of faith. We do, in fact, witness today, in the age of globalization, a growing sense of disorientation and isolation; we see, increasingly, a loss of meaning to life, an inability to connect with a "home" and a struggle to build meaningful relationships. It is therefore important to know how to dialogue and, with discernment, to use modern technologies and social networks in such a way as to reveal a presence that listens, converses, and encourages.

Allow yourselves, without fear, to be this presence, expressing your Christian identity as you become citizens of this environment.

— Address to the Plenary Assembly of the Pontifical Council for Social Communications, September 21, 2013

Reflection: How do we create cultures of dialogue online and offline? Pray for humility and an open heart.

"Put on Christ"

Jesus brings God to us and us to God. With him, our life is transformed and renewed, and we can see reality with new eyes, from Jesus' standpoint, with his own eyes (cf. *Lumen Fidei*, n. 18).

For this reason, I say to every one of you today: "Put on Christ!" in your life, and you will find a friend in whom you can always trust; "put on Christ," and you will see the wings of hope spreading and letting you journey with joy toward the future; "put on Christ," and your life will be full of his love; it will be a fruitful life. Because we all want to have a fruitful life, one that is life-giving for others.

— Address, World Youth Day, July 25, 2013

Reflection: Is your life transformed and renewed by Christ? Have you put on Christ as the center of your life?

Staying With the Lord

Jesus is the door, and he knocks on our door so that we will let him cross the threshold of our lives.... This means opening the doors of our hearts, like the disciples on the road to Emmaus did, asking him to stay with us so that we can pass through the door of faith, so that the Lord himself may bring us to the point where we understand our reasons for believing, and so that we can then go forth and proclaim him to others.

Faith implies a decision to stay with the Lord, to live with him, and to share him with our brothers and sisters.

— *Only Love Can Save Us*, Homily, October 1, 2012

Reflection: What does it mean to allow Jesus to cross the threshold of your life? Imagine your life as a house. What rooms do you let God into? Where do you keep him out? Have the courage to open your life to the Lord.

The Real Driving Force of Evangelization

Who is the real driving force of evangelization in our life and in the Church? Paul VI wrote clearly: "It is the Holy Spirit who today, just as at the beginning of the Church, acts in every evangelizer who allows himself to be possessed and led by him. The Holy Spirit places on his lips the words which he could not find by himself, and at the same time the Holy Spirit predisposes the soul of the hearer to be open and receptive to the Good News and to the Kingdom being proclaimed" (*Evangelii Nuntiandi*, n. 75).

— General Audience, May 22, 2013

Reflection: Are you "possessed" by the Holy Spirit? The Holy Spirit allows us to truly live out the Christian life. Don't ignore him. Don't put him aside. If you haven't asked the Holy Spirit to be in your life, ask him to be with you.

With Simplicity and Courage

Do not be afraid to live out faith! Be witnesses of Christ in your daily environment, with simplicity and courage. Above all, may you be able to show those you meet, your peers, the Face of mercy and the love of God who always forgives, encourages, and imbues hope.

— Message, June 21, 2013

Reflection: Ask God to lead you to situations today in which you can live out his mercy — by making room for someone in a conversation, for example, or generously forgiving a slight, or refusing to gossip.

Emptying Ourselves of Idols

We have to empty ourselves of the many small or great idols that we have and in which we take refuge, on which we often seek to base our security. They are idols that we sometimes keep well hidden; they can be ambition, careerism, a taste for success, placing ourselves at the center, the tendency to dominate others, the claim to be the sole masters of our lives, some sins to which we are bound, and many others.

— Homily, April 14, 2013

Reflection: Where do you find refuge apart from God? How does this give you a false security? Ask God to unbind you from these idols. Ask for the grace to break free and to place your hope in him.

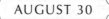

The Language of the Spirit

The language of the Spirit, the language of the Gospel, is the language of communion which invites us to get the better of closedness and indifference, division and antagonization. We must all ask ourselves: How do I let myself be guided by the Holy Spirit in such a way that my life and my witness of faith are both unity and communion? Do I convey the word of reconciliation and of love, which is the Gospel, to the milieus in which I live?

— General Audience, May 22, 2013

Reflection: Reflect on the questions Pope Francis asks above. How can you apply them to your everyday life and situation?

Responding to Evil With Good

Dear brothers and sisters, the word of the Cross is also the answer which Christians offer in the face of evil, the evil that continues to work in us and around us. Christians must respond to evil with good, taking the Cross upon themselves as Jesus did.

— Address, Way of the Cross, July 26, 2013

Reflection: Meditate for a few minutes on the love Jesus demonstrates on the Cross. So many people showed Jesus hatred and contempt, and yet he responds with love. What evil is God asking you to respond to with good?

Washing Feet

Our Lord's lucid and all-understanding awareness (knowing that the Father had put everything into his hands) leads him to gird himself with a towel and wash the feet of his disciples. A deeper and higher vision does not lead to new insights but to humble, specific, and concrete action.

— *Only Love Can Save Us*, First Regional Congress of
Urban Ministry in Buenos Aires, August 25, 2011

Reflection: Does an increase in your faith cause you to love more? Does it give you a greater humility or pride? Perform a specific and concrete act of humility this week.

Spiritual Combat

We must prepare ourselves for the spiritual combat. This is important. It is impossible to preach the Gospel without this spiritual battle, a daily battle against sadness, against bitterness, against pessimism; a daily battle!

— Address, June 17, 2013

Reflection: What gives you sadness, bitterness, and pessimism? God knows your battle. Ask God for the strength to overcome these struggles with his joy.

Pruning Our Language

There is no need to go to a psychiatrist to know that when people [put] someone else down, it is because they themselves are unable to develop and need to feel that the other is less important in order for them to feel that they count. [But Jesus said:] "Do not speak badly of others, do not belittle them, do not discredit them."

... It is not that we are wicked; we are weak and sinful.... It is far easier to solve a situation with an insult, with slander, with mud-slinging, rather than with kind words, as Jesus says.... [We must start by] pruning our language a little, by cutting back a bit our comments about others or the explosions that lead us to insulting them and flaring up in anger.

— Homily, Domus Sanctae Marthae, June 13, 2013

Reflection: Where are you tempted to gossip and speak ill of others? What is it about yourself that makes you prone to this? Ask God to help you improve in these areas so that you don't feel a need to use unkind words.

Living Consistently

It's not so much about speaking, but rather speaking with our whole lives: living consistently, the very consistency of our lives! This consistency means living Christianity as an encounter with Jesus that brings me to others, not just as a social label. In terms of society, this is how we are; we are Christians closed in on ourselves. No, not this! Witness is what counts!

— Address, Vigil of Pentecost With the
Ecclesial Movements, May 18, 2013

Reflection: As Christians, we can often segment our lives. We are Christians on Sunday at church, but not in the office on Monday. We are Christians when we are with our immediate family, but not with our friends at a party. Where do you lack consistency?

Blessed Mother Teresa of Calcutta

But one question remains: Where do we start? Whom do we ask to begin this work? Some people once asked Mother Teresa of Calcutta what needed to change in the Church, and which wall should they start with? They asked her, where is the starting point? And she replied, you and I are the starting point!

This woman showed determination! She knew where to start. And today I make her words my own, and I say to you: Shall we begin? Where? With you and me!

— Address, World Youth Day, July 27, 2013

Reflection: Ask yourself: If I must begin with myself, where exactly do I start? Open your heart so that Jesus may tell you where to start, and ask for the gift of determination to live it out.

He Is the One Hero!

The Gospel says that those seventy-two came back from their mission full of joy, because they had experienced the power of Christ's Name over evil. Jesus says it: To these disciples he gives the power to defeat the evil one. But he adds: "Do not rejoice in this, that the spirits are subject to you; but rejoice that your names are written in heaven" (Luke 10:20).

We should not boast as if we were the protagonists: there is only one protagonist; it is the Lord! The Lord's grace is the protagonist! He is the one hero! And our joy is just this: to be his disciples, his friends.

— Angelus address, July 7, 2013

Reflection: Reflect on your life and the accomplishments that you have achieved in the last few years. Give God the glory for each one. Ask God for the strength to journey more closely with him.

The Consumerist Model

The elderly ... are abandoned because of our selfish inability to accept their limitations, which reflect our own limitations. They are abandoned to the numerous pitfalls that must be overcome today to survive in a civilization that does not let them be active participants, have a voice, or serve as an example because the consumerist model dictates that "only youth has any use and only the youth can enjoy."

These elderly people are the very ones who, in society as a whole, should be a fount of wisdom of our people.

— *Only Love Can Save Us*, Homily, May 25, 2012

Reflection: Where does our culture's consumerist model affect you? Ask God to re-center your perspective, about yourself, others, and in particular the elderly and the sick.

Clouds of Indifference

We need to bring Christ to others, through these joys and hopes, like Mary, who brought Christ to the hearts of men and women; we need to pass through the clouds of indifference without losing our way; we need to descend into the darkest night without being overcome and disorientated; we need to listen to the dreams, without being seduced; we need to share their disappointments, without becoming despondent; to sympathize with those whose lives are falling apart, without losing our own strength and identity (cf. Pope Francis, Address to the Bishops of Brazil, July 27, 2013, n. 4).

This is the path. This is the challenge.

— Address, September 21, 2013

Reflection: To whom does Christ challenge you to go? How are you doing with this challenge? How can you find the Lord in this experience?

The Door of Our Lives

The new things of God, the trials of life, remaining steadfast in the Lord. Dear friends, let us open wide the door of our lives to the new things of God which the Holy Spirit gives us. May he transform us, confirm us in our trials, strengthen our union with the Lord, our steadfastness in him: this is a true joy! So may it be.

— Homily, Holy Mass With the Rite of Confirmation,
April 28, 2013

Reflection: What is God trying to tell you right now through your trials? How can you seek the Lord and draw closer to him during this time?

Don't Be Robbed of Hope

You know, it is easy to say don't lose hope. But to all, to you all, those who have work and those who don't, I say: "Do not let yourself be robbed of hope! Do not let yourselves be robbed of hope!" Perhaps hope is like embers under the ashes; let us help each other with solidarity, blowing on the ashes to rekindle the flame.

But hope carries us onward. That is not optimism; it is something else. However, hope does not belong to any one person; we all create hope! We must sustain hope in everyone, among all of you and among all of us who are far away. Hope is both yours and ours. It is something that belongs to everyone!

— Address, Meeting With Workers, September 22, 2013

Reflection: Do you know someone who needs hope and encouragement? Take time to pick up the phone and call this person.

Selfishness and Self-Absorption

Jesus is the incarnation of the Living God, the one who brings life amid so many deeds of death, amid sin, selfishness, and self-absorption. Jesus accepts, loves, uplifts, encourages, forgives, restores the ability to walk, gives back life.

— Homily, June 16, 2013

Reflection: With Jesus' example in mind, where is God calling you to encourage, forgive, and restore? Do you need God to encourage and restore you? Ask God to help you bring new life amid death, sin, and selfishness.

Walk Beside Jesus

Thinking that God is love does us so much good, because it teaches us to love, to give ourselves to others as Jesus gave himself to us and walks with us. Jesus walks beside us on the road through life.

— Angelus address, May 26, 2013

Reflection: Where can Jesus walk beside you this week? How can you walk beside him? How can you be his hands and feet?

Jesus Prefers Sinners

Jesus does not exclude anyone. Some of you, perhaps, might say to me: "But, Father, I am certainly excluded because I am a great sinner: I have done terrible things; I have done lots of them in my life." No, you are not excluded! Precisely for this reason, you are the favorite, because Jesus prefers sinners, always, in order to forgive them, to love them.

Jesus is waiting for you to embrace you, to pardon you. Do not be afraid: he is waiting for you.

— Angelus address, August 25, 2013

Reflection: What stops you from embracing Jesus and receiving his embrace?

What Happens Without the Cross?

FEAST OF THE EXALTATION OF THE HOLY CROSS

When we journey without the Cross, when we build without the Cross, when we profess Christ without the Cross, we are not disciples of the Lord, we are worldly: we may be bishops, priests, cardinals, popes, but not disciples of the Lord.

— Homily, March 14, 2013

Reflection: Why is the Cross essential to Christianity? Is the Cross essential to your own life? Do you use it as a lens to understand your sufferings? Do you have gratitude to the Lord because of it?

Complain to God

FEAST OF OUR LADY OF SORROWS

Lamenting to God is not a sin. A priest that I know once said to a woman who complained to God about her misfortunes: "Madam, that is a kind of prayer, go ahead. The Lord feels and hears our lamentations." [Job and Jeremiah] also lamented by cursing, not the Lord but the situation.... There are many people who are in these situations of existential suffering.... We [must think] about these people, whose suffering is so great, with our heart and with our flesh ... they must be an anxiety for me. My suffering brother, my suffering sister.

— Homily, Domus Sanctae Marthae, June 5, 2013

Reflection: First, tell God about your own sufferings. Second, ask for the grace to hear and help the sufferings of others.

Unearthing Hidden Idols

I am sure none of us stands before a tree to worship it as an idol ... none of us keeps statues to adore at home. [But] idolatry is subtle; we have our hidden idols, and the road through life to arrive at the Kingdom of God ... entails unearthing hidden idols.

— Homily, Domus Sanctae Marthae, June 6, 2013

Reflection: What idols do you need to unearth on your journey to the Kingdom of God? Pride? Wealth? Attention? What's one step or sacrifice you can make this week to separate yourself from your idols?

Rebel Against the Culture

Today, there are those who say that marriage is out of fashion. Is it out of fashion? In a culture of relativism and the ephemeral, many preach the importance of "enjoying" the moment. They say that it is not worth making a lifelong commitment, making a definitive decision, "forever," because we do not know what tomorrow will bring.

I ask you, instead, to be revolutionaries, I ask you to swim against the tide; yes, I am asking you to rebel against this culture that sees everything as temporary and that ultimately believes you are incapable of responsibility, that believes you are incapable of true love.

— Address, World Youth Day, July 28, 2013

Reflection: What commitments have you made to your family, parish, vocation, and friends? Make a firm resolution to stick to the commitments regardless of the cost, and ask God for the strength to do so.

Not an Enemy

My wish is that the dialogue between us should help to build bridges connecting all people, in such a way that everyone can see in the other not an enemy, not a rival, but a brother or sister to be welcomed and embraced!

— Address, March 22, 2013

Reflection: Whom do you view as an enemy or rival? How can you change your attitude? What action can you take this week to help you view this individual as a brother or sister?

Money

Money has to serve, not to rule! The Pope loves everyone, rich and poor alike, but the Pope has the duty, in Christ's name, to remind the rich to help the poor, to respect them, to promote them.

— Address, May 16, 2013

Reflection: When have you let the love of money overshadow your love of God? When have you let your love of God overshadow your love of money? Ask God to help you use your resources to serve others.

The Image of Christ and His Church

The Church is the bride. In the Gospel, [Jesus] returns many times to the images of the wise virgins waiting for the bridegroom with burning lamps and the feast that the father throws for the wedding of his son....

The Lord shows us that the relationship between him and the Church is matrimonial. This is the deepest reason why the Church guards the sacrament of Marriage. And it is called a great sacrament because it is precisely the image of the kind of union that Christ has with the Church.

— Homily, Domus Sanctae Marthae, September 6, 2013

Reflection: Throughout Scripture, God refers to his relationship with the People of God as matrimonial. In light of this, what is your love like for the Lord? Do you consider him the love of your life? Have you made a lifelong commitment to him?

Profound War Against Evil

It is the firm and courageous decision to renounce evil and its enticements and to choose the good, ready to pay in person: this is following Christ; this is what taking up our cross means!

This profound war against evil! What is the use of waging war, so many wars, if you aren't capable of waging this profound war against evil? It is pointless! It doesn't work.

— Angelus address, September 8, 2013

Reflection: If someone witnessed your day to day life, would they witness a battle against evil? What courageous actions would they see?

To Give Others a Few Blows

Gentleness is a somewhat forgotten virtue: being gentle, making room for others. There are so many enemies of gentleness, aren't there? Starting with gossip. When people prefer to tell tales, to gossip about others, to give others a few blows. These are daily events that happen to everyone, and to me too.... They are temptations of the evil one, who does not want the Spirit to create this gentleness in Christian communities.

— Homily, Domus Sanctae Marthae, April 9, 2013

Reflection: Once we gossip, our words are out there, never to be collected again. Take some time to examine your conscience and recall the times you have spoken poorly of others. Resolve to root out this temptation of the evil one and grow in the virtue of gentleness.

Jesus' Voice Is Unique

Jesus wants to establish with his friends a relationship which mirrors his own relationship with the Father: a relationship of reciprocal belonging in full trust, in intimate communion. To express this profound understanding, this relationship of friendship, Jesus uses the image of the shepherd with his sheep: he calls them and they recognize his voice; they respond to his call and follow him.

This parable is very beautiful! ... Jesus' voice is unique! If we learn to distinguish it, he guides us on the path of life, a path that goes beyond even the abyss of death.

— *Regina Caeli* address, April 14, 2013

Reflection: How do you hear the shepherd's voice? What other voices distract and deceive you in our world? In prayer, you can learn to distinguish the authentic voice of Jesus.

Welcome His Victory

Christ has fully triumphed over evil once and for all, but it is up to us, to the people of every epoch, to welcome this victory into our life and into the actual situations of history and society.

— *Regina Caeli* address, April 1, 2013

Reflection: In your trials, sufferings, and disappointments, remember Christ's victory. Invite the reality of Jesus' triumph into your life.

Grace

Of course, we must always have clearly in mind that we are justified, we are saved through grace, through an act of freely given love by God, who always goes before us; on our own, we can do nothing.

Faith is, first of all, a gift we have received. But in order to bear fruit, God's grace always demands our openness to him, our free and tangible response.

— General Audience, April 24, 2013

Reflection: What grace has God been offering to you lately? Where is he working and moving in your life? How can you open yourself up to this grace, in your heart, with your thoughts, and in your actions?

God Never Tires!
Let Us Never Tire!

Let us not forget this word: God never ever tires of forgiving us! "Well, Father, what is the problem?" Well, the problem is that we ourselves tire, we do not want to ask, we grow weary of asking for forgiveness. He never tires of forgiving, but at times we get tired of asking for forgiveness. Let us never tire; let us never tire!

He is the loving Father who always pardons, who has that heart of mercy for us all. And let us, too, learn to be merciful to everyone.

— Angelus address, March 17, 2013

Reflection: Do you grow weary of asking for forgiveness and of confessing the same sins? Let's accept the Lord's continual forgiveness, and let's continually forgive those who repeatedly offend us.

This Is Providence!

Jesus senses our problems, he senses our weaknesses, he senses our needs. Looking at those five loaves, Jesus thinks: This is Providence! From this small amount, God can make it suffice for everyone. Jesus trusts in the heavenly Father without reserve; he knows that for him everything is possible.

— Angelus address, June 2, 2013

Reflection: What are your weaknesses and needs? How do you think God is using these in his divine plan? Entrust your will to God's plan, however mysterious it may seem.

Justice and the Spiral of Evil

If we live according to the law "an eye for an eye, a tooth for a tooth," we will never escape from the spiral of evil. The evil one is clever, and deludes us into thinking that with our human justice we can save ourselves and save the world! In reality, only the justice of God can save us! And the justice of God is revealed in the Cross: the Cross is the judgment of God on us all and on this world.

But how does God judge us? By giving his life for us! Here is the supreme act of justice that defeated the prince of this world once and for all; and this supreme act of justice is the supreme act of mercy. Jesus calls us all to follow this path: "Be merciful, even as your Father is merciful" (Luke 6:36).

I now ask of you one thing. In silence, let's all think ... everyone think of a person with whom we are annoyed, with whom we are angry, someone we do not like. Let us think of that person and in silence, at this moment, let us pray for this person, and let us become merciful with this person.

— Angelus address, September 15, 2013

Reflection: Take some time in silence to act upon the Holy Father's request, above.

Who Is Like God?

Feast of Sts. Michael, Gabriel, and Raphael

Michael — which means: "Who is like God?" — is the champion of the primacy of God, of his transcendence and power. Michael fights to reestablish divine justice; he defends the People of God from their enemies and above all from the archenemy *par excellence*, the devil. And St. Michael triumphs because in him it is God who acts. This [St. Michael] sculpture reminds us, therefore, that evil is vanquished, the accuser is unmasked, his head is crushed, because salvation was fulfilled once and for all by the blood of Christ.

Even if the devil is always trying to scratch the face of the archangel and the face of man, God is stronger; his is the victory, and his salvation is offered to every human being.

— Address, July 5, 2013

Reflection: Do you call upon St. Michael to defend you in your battle against evil? And do you allow God to go before you in all you do, helping you to fight and to stand firm when you are in trouble? Make the choice to fight alongside him.

Common Sanctity

I see the holiness … in the patience of the People of God: a woman who is raising children, a man who works to bring home the bread, the sick, the elderly priests who have so many wounds but have a smile on their faces because they served the Lord, the sisters who work hard and live a hidden sanctity. This is for me the common sanctity.

I often associate sanctity with patience: not only patience as *hypomoné* [the New Testament Greek word], taking charge of the events and circumstances of life, but also as a constancy in going forward, day by day.

— Interview With Pope Francis, *America* magazine,
September 30, 2013

Reflection: Where is God calling you to be patient? How can you look to the Lord to find hope, meaning, and strength in times of routine or hard work? Trust in God, and allow him to move you forward.

Father

It is the Spirit himself, whom we received in Baptism, who teaches us, who spurs us to say to God: "Father" or, rather, "Abba!" — which means "papa" or ["dad"]. Our God is like this: he is a dad to us.... God treats us as children, he understands us, he forgives us, he embraces us, he loves us even when we err.

— General Audience, April 10, 2013

Reflection: We are children of the God of the universe, the one who is all-powerful and yet all-loving too. Does that fact make any difference to you as you go about your day-to-day life?

Guardian Angels

On the journey and in the trials of life, we are not alone: we are accompanied and sustained by the angels of God, who offer, so to speak, their wings to help us overcome the many dangers, to be able to fly above those realities that can make our lives difficult or drag us down.

— Address, July 5, 2013

Reflection: What role do angels play in your faith life? Catholics believe that each person has a guardian angel. Have you ever prayed to yours? Ask your guardian angel for help, protection, and guidance!

But It Isn't Easy!

Involvement in politics is an obligation for a Christian. We Christians cannot "play the role of Pilate," washing our hands of it; we cannot. We must be involved in politics because politics is one of the highest forms of charity, for it seeks the common good.

And Christian lay people must work in politics. You will say to me: "But it isn't easy!" Nor is it easy to become a priest. Nothing is easy in life.

— Address, To the Students of the Jesuit Schools of Italy and Albania, June 6, 2013

Reflection: For most of us, political involvement starts in our neighborhood and town. Are you active in the politics of your local community? How can you engage in both local and national politics in a way that seeks the common good?

Embracing the Suffering Body of Christ

FEAST OF ST. FRANCIS OF ASSISI

The young Francis abandoned riches and comfort in order to become a poor man among the poor. He understood that true joy and riches do not come from the idols of this world — material things and the possession of them — but are to be found only in following Christ and serving others.

Less well known, perhaps, is the moment when this understanding took concrete form in his own life. It was when Francis embraced a leper. This suffering brother was the "mediator of light ... for St. Francis of Assisi" (*Lumen Fidei*, n. 57), because in every suffering brother and sister that we embrace, we embrace the suffering Body of Christ.

— Address, World Youth Day, July 24, 2013

Reflection: Why is St. Francis' example important to us today? What does it mean for you to abandon your comfort and to embrace others?

Give Us This Merciful Heart

FEAST OF ST. FAUSTINA

God always wants mercy and does not condemn it in anyone. He wants heartfelt mercy because he is merciful and can understand well our misery, our difficulties, and also our sins. He gives all of us this merciful heart of his!

— Angelus address, July 14, 2013

Reflection: Jesus said, "Judge not, and you will not be judged; condemn not, and you will not be condemned; forgive, and you will be forgiven" (Luke 6:37). God establishes a relationship between our williness to give mercy to others and the mercy he gives to us. Who in your life needs forgiveness instead of judgment and condemnation?

Save Us From Being a Gnostic Church

The Holy Spirit draws us into the mystery of the living God and saves us from the threat of a Church which is gnostic and self-referential, closed in on herself; he impels us to open the doors and go forth to proclaim and bear witness to the good news of the Gospel, to communicate the joy of faith, the encounter with Christ.

— Homily, Mass With the Ecclesial Movements on Pentecost Sunday, May 19, 2013

Reflection: Do you communicate the joy of the faith, or do you project an air of anxiety or harshness or negativity? Fearlessly ask the Lord to help you see yourself as others see you, and to correct those things that hinder your witness.

To Overcome Egotism — Pray the Rosary

FEAST OF OUR LADY OF THE ROSARY

Here I would like to emphasize the beauty of a simple contemplative prayer, accessible to all, great and small, the educated and those with little education. It is the prayer of the Holy Rosary. In the Rosary, we turn to the Virgin Mary so that she may guide us to an ever closer union with her Son, Jesus, to bring us into conformity with him, to have his sentiments and to behave like him.

Indeed, in the Rosary, while we repeat the Hail Mary we meditate on the mysteries, on the events of Christ's life, so as to know and love him ever better. The Rosary is an effective means for opening ourselves to God, for it helps us to overcome egotism and to bring peace to hearts, in the family, in society, and in the world.

— Message, June 21, 2013

Reflection: Pray the Rosary today, focusing on the mysteries and imagining each scene and what it must have been like to be there. Pray for the wisdom to understand how these scenes relate to your own life.

God's World

God's world is a world where everyone feels responsible for the other, for the good of the other. This evening, in reflection, fasting, and prayer, each of us deep down should ask ourselves: Is this really the world that I desire? Is this really the world that we all carry in our hearts?

Is the world that we want really a world of harmony and peace, in ourselves, in our relations with others, in families, in cities, in and between nations? And does not true freedom mean choosing ways in this world that lead to the good of all and are guided by love?

— Vigil of Prayer for Peace, September 7, 2013

Reflection: Spend a few moments thinking about the pope's questions and their meaning for you.

Let Us Say "Yes"

The Living God sets us free! Let us say "yes" to love and not selfishness. Let us say "yes" to life and not death. Let us say "yes" to freedom and not enslavement to the many idols of our time. In a word, let us say "yes" to the God who is love, life, and freedom, and who never disappoints.

— Homily, June 16, 2013

Reflection: How can you reject selfishness, idols, and death and say "yes" to God today? What do you have to say "no" to today to make this "yes" possible?

What Has God Given You?

A Christian who withdraws into himself, who hides everything that the Lord has given him, is a Christian who ... he is not a Christian! He is a Christian who does not thank God for everything God has given him!

— General Audience, April 24, 2013

Reflection: Read the parable of the talents in Matthew 25:14-30. What talents has God given you? Are you using them or hiding them? Thank God by using the gifts he has given you.

The Fullness of Truth

As Jesus promised, the Holy Spirit guides us "into all the truth" (John 16:13); not only does he guide us to the encounter with Jesus, the fullness of the Truth, but he also guides us "into" the Truth — that is, he makes us enter into an ever deeper communion with Jesus, giving us knowledge of all the things of God. And we cannot achieve this by our own efforts.

Unless God enlightens us from within, our Christian existence will be superficial.

— General Audience, May 15, 2013

Reflection: Try reading one paragraph from the *Catechism* each day this week. See what you can learn about the truth of God.

New Leaven

Crossing the threshold of faith means trusting and acting in the power of the Holy Spirit, who is present in the Church and manifests himself in the signs of the times. It means joining in the constant flow of life and history without succumbing to the paralyzing defeatism that views past times as better. It is an urgency to think in new ways, offer new suggestions, and create new things, kneading life with the new leaven of "sincerity and truth" (1 Corinthians 5:8).

— *Only Love Can Save Us*, Letter to the Priests, Religious, and Faithful of Buenos Aires, October 1, 2012

Reflection: Have you ever caught yourself living in the past? How is God calling you to move on? How can you embrace the new opportunities that God presents to you?

The Mystery of the Eucharist

Let us ask ourselves: How do I follow Jesus? Jesus speaks in silence in the Mystery of the Eucharist. He reminds us every time that following him means going out of ourselves and not making our life a possession of our own, but rather a gift to him and to others.

— Homily, May 30, 2013

Reflection: Spend some time in Eucharistic adoration. Listen to what Jesus wants to tell you.

It Is to Your Advantage

Let us try asking ourselves: Am I open to the action of the Holy Spirit? Do I pray him to give me illumination, to make me more sensitive to God's things?

This is a prayer we must pray every day: "Holy Spirit, make my heart open to the Word of God, make my heart open to goodness, make my heart open to the beauty of God every day."

— General Audience, May 15, 2013

Reflection: Jesus said, "It is to your advantage that I go away, for if I do not go away, the Counselor will not come to you; but if I go, I will send him to you" (John 16:7). I invite the Holy Spirit to reign in your hearts, in your mind, and in your life today and every day.

A Soaking Wet Blanket

FEAST OF ST. TERESA OF JESUS

There is no holiness in sadness; there isn't any! St. Teresa ... said: "A saint who is sad is a sad saint." It is not worth much....

When you see a seminarian, a priest, a sister, or a novice with a long face, gloomy, who seems to have thrown a soaking wet blanket over their life, one of those heavy blankets ... which pulls one down.... Something has gone wrong! But please: never any sisters, never any priests with faces like "chilis pickled in vinegar" — never!

— Address, To Seminarians and Novices, July 6, 2013

Reflection: What is the relationship between holiness and joy? If you wish to have more joy, draw closer to our Lord. Put on joy, especially when others are wet blankets.

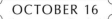

Faith Is Our Light

Whenever we let our thoughts, our feelings, or the logic of human power prevail, and we do not let ourselves be taught and guided by faith, by God, we become stumbling blocks. Faith in Christ is the light of our life as Christians!

— Homily, June 29, 2013

Reflection: God tells the prophet Isaiah that "as the heavens are higher than the earth, so are my ways higher than your ways and my thoughts than your thoughts" (Isaiah 55:9). We must use reason and logic to make decisions, but we must never forget to lead with faith and trust in God.

Understood and Loved

Throughout the Gospels, we see how Jesus by his words and actions brings the transforming life of God. This was the experience of the woman who anointed the feet of the Lord with ointment: she felt understood, loved, and she responded by a gesture of love: she let herself be touched by God's mercy, she obtained forgiveness, and she started a new life. God, the Living One, is merciful. Do you agree?

— Homily, June 16, 2013

Reflection: Where do you need transformation? Where do you need forgiveness and new life? Will you let God's mercy change you?

Is God Distant?

FEAST OF ST. LUKE

Our God is a God who is near, a God who makes himself present to us, a God who … became one of his people in Christ Jesus so that he could be close to us.

But it was not some kind of metaphysical closeness. Rather, it was the closeness that Luke describes when Jesus goes to heal the daughter of Jairus, where people crowded around him, almost suffocating him, while a poor little old lady at the back of the crowd struggled to touch the hem of his robe. It was the closeness of the crowd that wanted to silence the blind man at the entrance to Jericho who was trying to make himself heard by crying out. It is the closeness that gave courage to ten lepers to beg him to make them clean.

Jesus was into that kind of thing.

— *Only Love Can Save Us*, Homily, September 2, 2012

Reflection: Do you imagine God being distant from you or close? Reflect on the pope's words. What is holding you back from accepting God's desire to be close to you?

Listening to Our Daily Reality

This is also true in our life: listening to God, who speaks to us, and listening also to daily reality, paying attention to people, to events, because the Lord is at the door of our life and knocks in many ways, he puts signs on our path; he gives us the ability to see them.

— Address, May 31, 2013

Reflection: Use your time in prayer to reflect on your week. What signs is God putting in your path? What is he trying to tell you through the events, people, and places in your life?

The Law of Love

What is the law of the People of God? It is the law of love, love for God and love for neighbor, according to the new commandment that the Lord left to us (cf. John 13:34). It is a love, however, that is not sterile sentimentality or something vague, but the acknowledgment of God as the one Lord of life and, at the same time, the acceptance of the other as my true brother, overcoming division, rivalry, misunderstanding, selfishness; these two things go together. Oh, how much more of the journey do we have to make in order to actually live the new law.

— General Audience, June 12, 2013

Reflection: What do you struggle with more — loving God or loving your neighbor? Take time to work on any weakness in these areas this month. What is God calling you to do?

Becoming Instruments

Let us renew every day our trust in the Holy Spirit's action, the trust that he acts within us, that he is within us, that he gives us apostolic zeal, peace, and joy. Let us allow him to lead us. May we be men and women of prayer who witness to the Gospel with courage, becoming in our world instruments of unity and of communion with God.

— General Audience, May 22, 2013

Reflection: What kind of Christian are you today? What kind of Christian do you want to become? Ask God each day for the Holy Spirit to lead you to zeal, peace, joy, and prayer.

Wonder and Contemplation

Cultivating and caring for creation is an instruction of God which he gave not only at the beginning of history, but has also given to each one of us; ... Instead we are often guided by the pride of dominating, possessing, manipulating, and exploiting; we do not "preserve" the earth, we do not respect it, we do not consider it as a freely given gift to look after.

We are losing our attitude of wonder, of contemplation, of listening to creation.... Why does this happen? Why do we think and live horizontally? We have drifted away from God; we no longer read his signs.

— General Audience, June 5, 2013

Reflection: In your life, when do you tend to dominate, possess, manipulate, or exploit? How could wonder and contemplation help you in these areas?

Our True Treasure

Dear friends, let us keep the faith we have received and which is our true treasure; let us renew our faithfulness to the Lord, even in the midst of obstacles and misunderstanding. God will never let us lack strength and calmness.

— Homily, May 12, 2013

Reflection: What trials do you face that test your faith? How can you invite God into these situations? Where do you need strength?

Professing Christ Crucified

My wish is that all of us, after these days of grace, will have the courage, yes, the courage, to walk in the presence of the Lord, with the Lord's Cross; to build the Church on the Lord's blood, which was poured out on the Cross; and to profess the one glory: Christ crucified. And in this way, the Church will go forward.

— Homily, March 14, 2013

Reflection: The message of the Cross is one of love and sacrifice. How can you courageously profess this message to others in the routine actions of your life?

A Church With a Few Accidents

Jesus tells us: "Go into all the world! Go! Preach! Bear witness to the Gospel!" (cf. Mark 16:15). But what happens if we step outside ourselves? The same as can happen to anyone who comes out of the house and onto the street: an accident. But I tell you, I far prefer a Church that has had a few accidents to a Church that has fallen sick from being closed.

— Address, Vigil of Pentecost With the
Ecclesial Movements, May 18, 2013

Reflection: Do you feel vulnerable when you share your faith with others? Maybe you become nervous about what others will think or how they might react. But eternity is worth the awkwardness. Be courageous in sharing your faith with others.

As a Family, as Church

Let us ask ourselves today: How much do I love the Church? Do I pray for her? Do I feel part of the family of the Church? What do I do to ensure that she is a community in which each one feels welcome and understood, feels the mercy and love of God who renews life?

Faith is a gift and an act which concern us personally, but God calls us to live with our faith together, as a family, as Church.

— General Audience, May 29, 2013

Reflection: Sometimes our Church can be hard to love. Do you have an issue with a teaching of the Church? Try to learn more about it. Do you have a problem with a specific person within the Church? Work on forgiving him or her.

What Does It Mean to Worship God?

What does it mean, then, to worship God? It means learning to be with him, it means that we stop trying to dialogue with him, and it means sensing that his presence is the most true, the most good, the most important thing of all.

— Homily, April 14, 2013

Reflection: Begin your time in prayer by asking God to be present to you. Spend at least five minutes in silence, meditating on his presence.

Hide My Sin in Your Wounds

In my own life, I have so often seen God's merciful countenance, his patience; I have also seen so many people find the courage to enter the wounds of Jesus by saying to him: Lord, I am here, accept my poverty, hide my sin in your wounds, wash it away with your blood. And I have always seen that God did just this — he accepted them, consoled them, cleansed them, loved them.

— Homily, Divine Mercy Sunday, April 7, 2013

Reflection: Your sins are not too big for God's mercy. Trust in him. Ask him for forgiveness. Ask him to make you clean. Take part in the sacrament of Penance.

Faith Is Strengthened by Proclamation

Are we capable of bringing the Word of God into the environment in which we live? Do we know how to speak of Christ, of what he represents for us, in our families, among the people who form part of our daily lives? Faith is born from listening and is strengthened by proclamation.

— Homily, April 14, 2013

Reflection: Do you know how to speak of Christ? To proclaim the Gospel with actions and words? Who in your life can help you learn to proclaim Christ to others?

Closest to His Heart

For God, we are not numbers, we are important, indeed we are the most important thing to him; even if we are sinners, we are what is closest to his heart.

— Homily, Divine Mercy Sunday, April 7, 2013

Reflection: Jesus said, "Are not five sparrows sold for two pennies? And not one of them is forgotten before God. Why, even the hairs of your head are all numbered. Fear not; you are of more value than many sparrows" (Luke 12:6-8). In prayer, open yourself to the intimate relationship God wants to have with you.

From Sinners to Saints

If we — all of us — accept the grace of Jesus Christ, he changes our heart and from sinners makes us saints. To become holy, we do not need to turn our eyes away and look somewhere else, or have, as it were, the face on a holy card! No, no, that is not necessary.

To become saints, only one thing is necessary: to accept the grace which the Father gives us in Jesus Christ.

— Address, June 17, 2013

Reflection: For you, what does it mean to be a saint? Do you think it is possible for you to be a saint here on earth? Pray about those areas that hold you back from that goal, and ask for God's grace to help you.

The Middle Class of Holiness

Feast of All Saints

To be sure, the testimony of faith comes in very many forms, just as in a great fresco, there is a variety of colors and shades; … In God's great plan, every detail is important, even yours, even my humble little witness, even the hidden witness of those who live their faith with simplicity in everyday family relationships, work relationships, friendships.

There are the saints of every day, the "hidden" saints, a sort of "middle class of holiness," as a French author said, that "middle class of holiness" to which we can all belong.

— Homily, April 14, 2013

Reflection: How can your family relationships, work relationships, and friendships be a means to help you grow closer to the Lord? How can you find holiness in your everyday routine as a member of the "middle class of holiness"?

Never Lose Hope

ALL SOULS' DAY

May conflict that sows death make room for encounter and reconciliation that bring life. To all who are suffering I say forcefully: Never lose hope! The Church is beside you, accompanies you, and sustains you!

— Address, June 20, 2013

Reflection: Pray for the people in your life who have passed away, remembering with gratitude any good examples they set for you. Pray for those throughout the world who have died with no one to care about or pray for them.

Devotions, But No Jesus

[Today] we encounter many Christians without Christ. For example, those like the Pharisees, Christians who put their faith, their religiosity, their Christianity, in laws: I must do this, I must do that. They are Christians out of habit.... [They] seek out only devotions, but no Jesus.

There is something missing, my brother! Jesus is missing. If your devotions lead you to Jesus, then they are good. But if they leave you where you are, then something is wrong.

— Homily, Domus Sanctae Marthae, September 7, 2013

Reflection: Ask yourself: "Is my faith primarily a matter of laws and habit? What can I do to more decisively put Jesus at the center of my devotions, and my time at Mass?" Consciously re-center all of your activities on Jesus.

The Only One Who Can Make Something New

Jesus has the power, through the power of his Spirit, to renew hearts. We need to be confident of this. If we do not trust in Jesus' power as the only means of salvation, if we do not trust that he is the only one who can make something new, we are false Christians. We are not truly Christian.

— *Only Love Can Save Us*, Homily, February 18, 2012

Reflection: Do you trust in Jesus' power? Do you think he can really renew your heart? Do you believe he is the only means of salvation? Ask Jesus to give you faith.

Sterile and Incomplete Prayer

In our Christian life too, dear brothers and sisters, may prayer and action always be deeply united. A prayer that does not lead you to practical action for your brother — the poor, the sick, those in need of help, a brother in difficulty — is a sterile and incomplete prayer.

But, in the same way, when ecclesial service is attentive only to doing, things gain in importance, functions, structures, and we forget the centrality of Christ. When time is not set aside for dialogue with him in prayer, we risk serving ourselves and not God present in our needy brother and sister.

— Angelus address, July 21, 2013

Reflection: Does your prayer involve both dialogue and practical action? Talk to Jesus. Listen to him. Write down what he is asking you to do, and then live it out.

A Race

Man's life on earth is warfare; Job says it, meaning that people are constantly put to the test; that is to say, a test to overcome a situation and overcome oneself. St. Paul took it and applied it to athletes that compete in an arena and who must deny themselves many things in order to achieve success.

The Christian life is also a sort of sport, a struggle, a race, where one has to detach oneself from the things that separate us from God.

— *On Heaven and Earth: Pope Francis on Faith, Family, and the Church in the 21st Century*

Reflection: In the First letter to the Corinthians, St. Paul compares the Christian to an athlete competing for a prize (see 1 Corinthians 9:24-27). What goal are you running toward? Where do you need self-control? How hard are you running?

The Road We Have Traveled

To remember what God has done and continues to do for me, for us, to remember the road we have traveled; this is what opens our hearts to hope for the future. May we learn to remember everything that God has done in our lives.

— Homily, Easter Vigil, March 30, 2013

Reflection: Recall what God has done throughout your life. Keep this in mind as you talk to God about his plans for your future.

Listening Attentively

Listening is not simply hearing. Listening is being attentive. Listening is the desire to understand, to value, to respect, and to save. We must find the means to listen attentively so that each person may speak and so that we are aware of what each person wishes to say.

— *Only Love Can Save Us*, Homily, August 7, 2006

Reflection: Practice truly listening to people. Try to understand where they are coming from and why they feel the way they do. Start by attentively listening to God in prayer and trying to understand what he says to you.

The Righteous Man Ponders

Instead of thinking about what others may owe us, let's think about what we owe to others. This adds to a person's dignity: the righteous man ponders how he can be even more just. He does so without anyone forcing him. He does it for the honor and the pleasure that comes from being righteous, from giving back what is not his, from offering reparation to those whom he has cheated.

— *Only Love Can Save Us*, Homily, August 7, 2011

Reflection: The virtue of justice is centered on what we owe others. What do you owe others at home, at work, and in your community? Where are you currently fulfilling your obligations? Where can you improve?

The Lethargy of Good People

Some might say: "But, Father, how can we bring love to a global civilization, which amid its many contradictions, seems to be set on an apocalyptic course? How can we care for life from beginning to end?" The great Pope Pius XI once said something very challenging: "It is not the negative forces of civilization that are the great problem of our time, but rather the lethargy of its good people."

— *Only Love Can Save Us*, Homily, Feast of the Annunciation, March 25, 2011

Reflection: In what situations are you lethargic? What keeps you from acting? Take a step toward making a difference in this area today.

He Sees the Son From Afar

I am always struck when I reread the parable of the merciful Father [Luke 15:11-32].... And the Father? Had he forgotten the son? No, never. He is there, he sees the son from afar, he was waiting for him every hour of every day; the son was always in his father's heart, even though he had left him, even though he had squandered his whole inheritance, his freedom.

The Father, with patience, love, hope, and mercy, had never for a second stopped thinking about him, and as soon as he sees him still far off, he runs out to meet him and embraces him with tenderness.

— Homily, Divine Mercy Sunday, April 7, 2013

Reflection: Think about a time you committed a sin. How do you think God looked upon you in that moment? How does this compare to the image in the parable of the merciful Father? How does this perspective change the way you ask for mercy and forgiveness?

Lord of Consolation

Do not be afraid, because the Lord is the Lord of consolation, he is the Lord of tenderness. The Lord is a Father, and he says that he will be for us like a mother with her baby, with a mother's tenderness. Do not be afraid of the consolations of the Lord.

— Homily, June 29, 2013

Reflection: Where do you need to be consoled? Talk to God about the trials and difficulties in your life.

How Beautiful It Is

There is no time to be lost in gossip, there is no need to wait for everyone's consensus; what is necessary is to go out and proclaim. To all people you bring the peace of Christ, and if they do not welcome it, you go ahead just the same. To the sick you bring healing, because God wants to heal man of every evil.

How many missionaries do this! They sow life, health, comfort, to the outskirts of the world. How beautiful it is! Do not live for yourselves, do not live for yourselves, but live to go forth and do good!

— Angelus address, July 7, 2013

Reflection: On a practical level, what does it look like in your everyday life when you live for others and not for yourself? Where are you moving forward in regard to leaving selfishness behind? Don't let anything hold you back — bring the Gospel to others.

Always Destruction

The devil is … a being that opted not to accept the plan of God.… Jesus defines him as the Father of Lies.… His fruits are always destruction: division, hate, and slander. And in my personal experience, I feel him every time that I am tempted to do something that is not what God wants for me.

I believe that the devil exists. Maybe his greatest achievement in these times has been to make us believe that he does not exist.

— *On Heaven and Earth: Pope Francis on Faith, Family, and the Church in the 21st Century*

Reflection: Do you believe that the devil exists? In what area of your life is he trying to tempt you? How are you fighting this temptation? Trust in God that he will help you to choose his plan over the devil's.

Communion of Saints

Be aware of the companionship of the whole Church and also the communion of the saints on this mission. When we face challenges together, then we are strong; we discover resources we did not know we had. Jesus did not call the apostles to live in isolation; he called them to form a group, a community.

— Homily, World Youth Day, Closing Mass, July 28, 2013

Reflection: Have you chosen a saint to be a friend, patron, model, and intercessor for you? Learn more about that saint this week, and ask him or her to help you with specific challenges you're facing now.

The God-Money Idol

God did not want an idol to be at the center of the world but man, men and women who would keep the world going with their work. Yet now, in this system devoid of ethics, at the center there is an idol, and the world has become an idolater of this "god-money." Money is in command! Money lays down the law! It orders all these things that are useful to it, this idol.

And what happens? To defend this idol, all crowd to the center, and those on the margins are done down, the elderly fall away, because there is no room for them in this world!

— Address, Meeting With Workers, September 22, 2013

Reflection: Where do you see this "god-money" as an idol in our culture? How does it become an idol in your own life? What's one practical step you can take to fight against this idol during the upcoming week?

Parresia

We must pray with *parresia* — with courage, boldness, and confidence. We cannot sit still after having prayed once. True Christian intercession consists of insisting to the very end.

— *Only Love Can Save Us*, Letter to Priests and Religious,
July 29, 2007

Reflection: What are you praying for right now? Take up the pope's challenge and pray with greater boldness and consistency.

Does the Truth Really Exist?

We are living in an age in which people are rather skeptical of truth. Benedict XVI has frequently spoken of relativism — that is, of the tendency to consider nothing definitive and to think that truth comes from consensus or from something we like.

The question arises: Does "the" truth really exist? What is "the" truth? Can we know it? Can we find it? ... It is the Holy Spirit himself, the gift of the Risen Christ, who makes us recognize the Truth.

— General Audience, May 15, 2013

Reflection: Have you found it difficult to trust in truth in a culture of relativism? What helps you hold fast to the truth? In what situations are you tempted to relativize? Invite the Holy Spirit to be with you, to go with you, and to help you recognize truth.

How Can We Let Jesus Out?

But ask yourselves this question: How often is Jesus inside and knocking at the door to be let out, to come out? And we do not let him out because of our own need for security, because so often we are locked into ephemeral structures that serve solely to make us slaves and not free children of God.

— Address, Vigil of Pentecost With the
Ecclesial Movements, May 18, 2013

Reflection: Where do you turn for comfort? How can you move beyond comfort to seek out the plan Jesus has for you? How can you let Jesus out?

Proclaim the Gospel —
This Includes You

Jesus did not say: "Go, if you would like to, if you have the time," but he said: "Go and make disciples of all nations." Sharing the experience of faith, bearing witness to the faith, proclaiming the Gospel: this is a command that the Lord entrusts to the whole Church, and that includes you.

— Homily, World Youth Day, Closing Mass, July 28, 2013

Reflection: What excuses do you make in order to avoid sharing your faith with others? How is the Lord calling you to make disciples?

Absurd Dichotomy

The great Paul VI said: It is an absurd dichotomy to wish to live with Jesus but without the Church, to follow Jesus but without the Church, to love Jesus but without the Church (cf. *Evangelii Nuntiandi*, n. 16). And that Mother Church who gives us Jesus also gives us an identity which is not simply a rubber stamp: it is membership. Identity means membership, belonging. Belonging to the Church: this is beautiful!

— Homily, April 23, 2013

Reflection: Jesus established the Kingdom of God here on earth in the form of the Church (see Matthew 16:13-20). How does believing in both Jesus and his Church shape your life? What does it mean for you to belong to this Church, this kingdom?

Faithful

It is not creativity, however pastoral it may be, or meetings or planning that ensure our fruitfulness, even if these are greatly helpful. But what assures our fruitfulness is our being faithful to Jesus.

— Homily, World Youth Day, July 27, 2013

Reflection: Your daily meeting with God in prayer is more important than anything else. It is from this that your faithfulness and success flow.

Sixty Years With Jesus

Yesterday I celebrated the sixtieth anniversary of the day when I heard Jesus' voice in my heart. I am telling you this not so that you will make me a cake here, no, that is not why I'm saying it. However, it is a commemoration: sixty years since that day. I will never forget it. The Lord made me strongly aware that I should take that path.

I was seventeen years old. Several years passed before this decision, this invitation, became concrete and definitive. So many years have gone by, with some successes and joys but so many years with failures, frailties, sin ... sixty years on the Lord's road, behind him, beside him, always with him. I only tell you this: I have no regrets! I have no regrets! Why? Because I feel like Tarzan and I feel strong enough to go ahead? No, I have not regretted it because always, even at the darkest moments, the moments of sin and moments of frailty, moments of failure, I have looked at Jesus and trusted in him, and he has not deserted me. Trust in Jesus: he always keeps on going, he goes with us!

— Address, Meeting With Young People, September 22, 2013

Reflection: Do you have a moment in your life when you made a commitment to Jesus as Pope Francis did? Where has Jesus been with you on this journey since then? What do these experiences mean to you?

What Kind of King?

But what kind of a king is Jesus? Let us take a look at him: he is riding on a donkey, he is not accompanied by a court, he is not surrounded by an army as a symbol of power. He is received by humble people, simple folk who have the sense to see something more in Jesus.

— Homily, March 24, 2013

Reflection: What is the relationship between your simplicity and your ability to accept Jesus? What is Jesus asking you to put aside to receive him? Where is Jesus asking you to be humble so that you are more like him?

He Asked for Nothing

God thinks like the Samaritan who did not pass by the unfortunate man, pitying him or looking at him from the other side of the road, but helped him without asking for anything in return; without asking whether he was a Jew, a pagan, or a Samaritan, whether he was rich or poor: he asked for nothing. He went to help him: God is like this. God thinks like the shepherd who lays down his life in order to defend and save his sheep.

— General Audience, March 27, 2013

Reflection: How does God exceed our understanding of love and forgiveness? In what ways have you seen him go above and beyond your expectations to help *you?* How can you live out this model of mercy?

I Don't Have Time

Someone might say to me: "But Father, I don't have time," "I have so many things to do," "It's difficult," "What can I do with my feebleness and my sins, with so many things?" We are often satisfied with a few prayers, with a distracted and sporadic participation in Sunday Mass, with a few charitable acts; but we do not have the courage "to come out" to bring Christ to others.

— General Audience, March 27, 2013

Reflection: Our understanding of time is relative to our desires. We don't have time for many important things, but we are distracted by trivial forms of media that waste our time and don't fulfill us. Where do you need to make time for God? Where does he want you to serve?

Illusions of Happiness

Jesus is all mercy, Jesus is all love: he is God made man. Each of us, each one of us, is that little lost lamb, the coin that was mislaid; each one of us is that son who has squandered his freedom on false idols, illusions of happiness, and has lost everything. But God does not forget us; the Father never abandons us. He is a patient father, always waiting for us! He respects our freedom, but he remains faithful forever.

And when we come back to him, he welcomes us like children into his house, for he never ceases, not for one instant, to wait for us with love. And his heart rejoices over every child who returns. He is celebrating because he is joy. God has this joy, when one of us sinners goes to him and asks his forgiveness.

— Angelus address, September 15, 2013

Reflection: Consider the times that God has rescued you from your sin — in your childhood, in your adolescence, in your adulthood. Thank him for the grace you have received, and think about the aspects of your life that still need to return to him.

Not a Cultural Organization

We can do all the social work we like, and people can say: "How good the Church is, what good social work the Church does!" But if we say we do this because those people are the flesh of Christ, it gives rise to a scandal....

The Church is not a cultural or religious organization, nor is it a social one; it is not this. The Church is the family of Jesus. The Church confesses that Jesus is the Son of God who came in flesh. This is the scandal, and this is why they persecuted Jesus.... If we become merely reasonable, social and charitable Christians, what will the consequence be? That we will never have martyrs....

[But when we say] the Son of God came and became flesh, when we preach the scandal of the Cross, there will be persecution, there will be the Cross. [Do not] be ashamed of living with this scandal of the Cross.
— Homily, Domus Sanctae Marthae, June 1, 2013

Reflection: What is the difference between someone who lives a cultural faith and someone who confesses that Jesus is the Son of God who came in the flesh? How would they talk and live differently? If someone witnessed your life, what would they say about you?

Even If We Observe All of His Precepts

If in our heart there is no mercy, no joy of forgiveness, we are not in communion with God, even if we observe all of his precepts, for it is love that saves, not the practice of precepts alone. It is love of God and neighbor that brings fulfillment to all the commandments. And this is the love of God, his joy: forgiveness. He waits for us always! Maybe someone has some heaviness in his heart: "But, I did this, I did that...." He expects you! He is your father: he waits for you always!

— Angelus address, September 15, 2013

Reflection: It is good to do the right thing, but ultimately God wants your heart. Think about the upcoming week. Where is God calling you, not only to do the right thing but to do it with love as well?

Don't Be Distracted

I would tell the people of today to seek the experience of entering into the intimacy of their hearts, to know the experience, the face of God. That is why I love what Job says after his difficult experience and the dialogues that did not help him in any way: "By hearsay I had heard of you, but now my eye has seen you" (Job 42:5).

What I tell people is not to know God only by hearing. The Living God is he that you may see with your eyes within your hearts.

— On Heaven and Earth: Pope Francis on Faith, Family, and the Church in the 21st Century

---

Reflection: Where have you seen God in the past? How do you experience him today? Find extra time this week to seek the face of God. Perhaps schedule a retreat — even just an afternoon — to spend more time with him.

Cultivate the Contemplative Dimension

If we look toward Jesus, we see that prior to any important decision or event he recollected himself in intense and prolonged prayer. Let us cultivate the contemplative dimension, even amid the whirlwind of more urgent and heavy duties. And the more the mission calls you to go out to the margins of existence, let your heart be the more closely united to Christ's heart, full of mercy and love.

— Homily, Mass With Seminarians and Novices, July 7, 2013

Reflection: What important decisions are before you right now? How can you draw closer to Jesus as you sort things out? Take time as you wake, in your prayer, in your thoughts throughout the day, and before bed to ask God to guide your path.

You Do Not Need Anything Else

What must we do, Father? Look, read the Beatitudes: that will do you good. If you want to know what you actually have to do, read Matthew, chapter 25, which is the standard by which we will be judged. With these two things, you have the action plan: the Beatitudes and Matthew 25. You do not need to read anything else.

— Address, World Youth Day, July 25, 2013

Reflection: Read the Beatitudes in Matthew 5:1-12 and the Last Judgment scene in Matthew 25:31-46. What stood out to you? What spoke to your life right now? Make a resolution to try to live out your insight this month.

Who Is Against Us?

Even though it seems today that death in its various forms prevails, that history is governed by the rule of the strongest (or the cleverest), and that hatred and ambition are the driving forces behind so much human strife, we are also utterly convinced that this sorry situation ultimately can and must change, because "If God is for us, who is against us?" (Romans 8:31).

— *Only Love Can Save Us*, Letter to the Priests, Religious, and Faithful of Buenos Aires, October 1, 2012

Reflection: When faced with the attitudes and actions of hatred and ambition, are you tempted to fight back with evil? Do you sometimes despair? Talk with God about the times you feel helpless. Reflect on the times in Scripture when situations seemed dire or hopeless. Ask God to see the world through his eyes and in his presence.

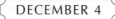
Earthly Pilgrimage

Let us ask the Lord always to direct our minds and hearts to him, as living stones of the Church, so that all that we do, our whole Christian life, may be a luminous witness to his mercy and love. In this way we will make our way toward the goal of our earthly pilgrimage, toward that extremely beautiful shrine, the heavenly Jerusalem.

— Homily, Holy Mass With the Rite of Confirmation,
April 28, 2013

Reflection: What path are you walking on? Are others able to see this path — for good or ill — through your example?

Do Not Be Afraid!

You were also talking about the fragility of faith, about how to overcome it. The worst enemy of a fragile faith — curious, isn't it? — is fear. Do not be afraid! We are frail and we know it, but he is stronger! If you walk with him, there is no problem! A child is very frail — I have seen many children today — but if they're with their father, with their mother, they are safe. With the Lord we are safe.

— Address, Vigil of Pentecost With the
Ecclesial Movements, May 18, 2013

Reflection: What do you fear? What keeps you up at night? Ask God to replace your fears with the joy of knowing his presence.

You Are Important to Me

FEAST OF ST. NICHOLAS

True joy does not come from things or from possessing, no! It is born from the encounter, from the relationship with others; it is born from feeling accepted, understood, and loved, and from accepting, from understanding and from loving; and this is not because of a passing fancy but because the other is a person.

Joy is born from the gratuitousness of an encounter! It is hearing someone say, but not necessarily with words: "You are important to me." This is beautiful. . . . And it is these very words that God makes us understand. In calling you, God says to you: "You are important to me, I love you, I am counting on you." Jesus says this to each one of us! Joy is born from that!

— Address, To Seminarians and Novices, July 6, 2013

Reflection: In a season of possessions and gifts, how can you give the gift of presence to others? What steps can you take to let others know they are important to you?

The Latest Smartphone

Some will say: Joy is born from possessions, so they go in quest of the latest model of the smartphone, the fastest scooter, the showy car ... but I tell you, it truly grieves me to see a priest or a sister with the latest model of a car: but this can't be! It can't be. You think: "So, do we now have to go by bicycle, Father? Bicycles are good! Monsignor Alfred rides a bicycle. He goes by bike.

I think that cars are necessary because there is so much work to be done, and also in order to get about ... but choose a more humble car! And if you like the beautiful one, only think of all the children who are dying of hunger.

— Address, To Seminarians and Novices, July 6, 2013

Reflection: Scripture says, "For where your treasure is, there will your heart be also" (Luke 12:34). What is your ultimate treasure, and where is your heart right now?

Mary Knew How to Listen

FEAST OF THE IMMACULATE CONCEPTION

Mary knew how to listen to God. Be careful: it was not merely "hearing," a superficial word, but it was "listening," that consists of attention, acceptance, and availability to God. It was not in the distracted way with which we sometimes face the Lord or others: we hear their words, but we do not really listen. Mary is attentive to God. She listens to God.

— Address, May 31, 2013

Reflection: Mary listened attentively to the angel Gabriel when she was asked to be the mother of God. Attentive to the needs of her cousin Elizabeth, she went to her when Elizabeth needed help. She contemplated the events of the Nativity in her heart. What can you learn from Mary's witness? How does God want you to live this out this season of Advent?

That Is What God Is Like

God does not wait for us to go to him, but it is he who moves toward us, without calculation, without quantification. That is what God is like. He always takes the first step; he comes toward us.

— General Audience, March 27, 2013

Reflection: Where is God calling you to be like him and to take the first step toward others? Do you need to reconcile with someone? Do you need to show an act of kindness to someone in your life?

He Shares in Our Journey

Jesus ... gives himself to us in the Eucharist, shares in our journey, indeed he makes himself food, the true food that sustains our life also in moments when the road becomes hard going and obstacles slow our steps. And in the Eucharist, the Lord makes us walk on his road, that of service, of sharing, of giving; and if it is shared, that little we have, that little we are, becomes riches, for the power of God — which is the power of love — comes down into our poverty to transform it.

— Homily, May 30, 2013

Reflection: Pray in front of the Eucharist for fifteen minutes this week. Ask God to transform you through this great sacrament.

He Pitched His Tent Among Us

God came out of himself to come among us, he pitched his tent among us to bring to us his mercy that saves and gives hope. Nor must we be satisfied with staying in the pen of the ninety-nine sheep, if we want to follow him and to remain with him; we, too, must "go out" with him to seek the lost sheep, the one that has strayed the furthest. Be sure to remember: coming out of ourselves, just as Jesus, just as God came out of himself in Jesus and Jesus came out of himself for all of us.

— General Audience, March 27, 2013

Reflection: The Letter to the Philippians speaks of Jesus emptying himself for us and becoming a servant (see Philippians 2:5-8). What can you learn from Christ's example? How is he asking you to come out of yourself for the sake of others?

Entrusting the Church to the Lord

FEAST OF OUR LADY OF GUADALUPE

To pray for the Church will do us good, and it will benefit the Church; it will bring great peace in us; it may not remove our trials, but it will make us strong. Thus, let us beg for this grace to have the habit of entrusting the Church to the Lord.

— Homily, Domus Sanctae Marthae, April 30, 2013

Reflection: What can you do to lift up your parish, religious sisters and brothers, your pastor, bishop, and pope in prayer? Can you add them to your intentions each day? Be at peace knowing they are in the Lord's hands.

The Highway of Our Lives

This evening I would like a question to resound in the heart of each one of you, and I would like you to answer it honestly: Have I considered which idol lies hidden in my life that prevents me from worshiping the Lord? Worshiping is stripping ourselves of our idols, even the most hidden ones, and choosing the Lord as the center, as the highway of our lives.

— Homily, April 14, 2013

Reflection: Take some time to think about Pope Francis' question: Have you considered which idol lies hidden in your life that prevents you from worshiping the Lord?

Contemplate Beauty and Goodness

But then we wonder: Is this the world in which we are living? Creation retains its beauty, which fills us with awe, and it remains a good work. But there is also "violence, division, disagreement, war." This occurs when man, the summit of creation, stops contemplating beauty and goodness, and withdraws into his own selfishness.

— Vigil of Prayer for Peace, September 7, 2013

Reflection: Take some time this week to contemplate God's beauty and goodness. Go on a hike. Take a drive in a scenic area. Be filled with awe. Contemplate beauty.

Not Decorating Life With a Little Religion

Jesus says to his disciples: "Do you think that I have come to give peace on earth? No, I tell you, but rather division" (Luke 12:51). What does this mean? It means that faith is not a decorative or ornamental element; living faith does not mean decorating life with a little religion, as if it were a cake and we were decorating it with cream. No, this is not faith.

Faith means choosing God as the criterion and basis of life — and God is not empty, God is not neutral, God is always positive, God is love, and love is positive!

— Angelus address, August 11, 2013

Reflection: In this season of Advent, consider those areas in which your faith is merely ornamental. How can you make God the basis of your life, and not just something decorative? Cut out the things that only distract or take away from your focus on him.

Where Is Grace Sold?

Is there any one of you who knows what grace costs? Where grace is sold? Where I can purchase grace? No one can answer: no. Do I go to buy it from the parish office; perhaps grace is sold there? Does some priest sell grace?

Listen to this carefully: Grace is neither bought nor sold; it is a gift of God in Jesus Christ. Jesus Christ gives us grace. He is the only one who gives us grace. It is a present: he is offering it to us, to us. Let us accept it.

— Address, June 17, 2013

Reflection: In order to receive God's grace, we must make room for Jesus in our heart, letting him become more as we become less. But how do we accept God's grace? The sacraments are one means — we receive God's very self in the Eucharist, and we are forgiven by Christ himself in the sacrament of Penance.

He Has Been Tempted as We Are

How many difficulties are present in the life of every individual, among our people, in our communities; yet as great as these may seem, God never allows us to be overwhelmed by them. In the face of those moments of discouragement we experience in life, in our efforts to evangelize or to embody our faith as parents within the family, I would like to say forcefully: Always know in your heart that God is by your side; he never abandons you!

Let us never lose hope! Let us never allow it to die in our hearts!

— Homily, World Youth Day, July 24, 2013

Reflection: Where do you feel overwhelmed or discouraged? Scripture says that "we have not a high priest who is unable to sympathize with our weaknesses, but one who in every respect has been tempted as we are, yet without sinning" (Hebrews 4:15). Talk to Jesus about the challenges you face, knowing that he went through many trials himself.

May His Mercy Enter

Let us ask Jesus now for the grace to open our hearts so that his mercy may enter. Let's say, "Yes, Lord, I am a sinner. I am a sinner because of this and because of that. Come, come and justify me before the Father."
— *Only Love Can Save Us*, Homily, September 24, 2011

Reflection: An examination of conscience is a beautiful tradition in the Church. Find a guide to this practice in a book, online, or at your parish, and use it each day this week. See if it helps you draw near to Jesus.

To Become Incarnate

[Jesus] seems to show no mercy to those who have taken ... the reality of a God who is close, God who is walking with his people, who became man ... and distilled it along with their many traditions and made it simply an idea, purely a precept, thereby alienating so many people. Indeed, Jesus will accuse these people of being proselytizers, of proselytizing. They go halfway around the world to look for someone to proselytize, and then they burden them with all their laws and precepts. They alienate people....

Jesus taught us another way: that of going out — going out to give witness, going out to take a concern for brothers and sisters, going out to share, going out to inquire. To become incarnate.

— *Only Love Can Save Us*, Homily, September 2, 2012

Reflection: What is the difference between someone who makes Jesus into just an idea versus someone who shares the faith by going out and encountering others? What do their lives look like? How can you avoid making Jesus into a set of rules and instead let him be as he is, a reality?

He Always Makes Himself Heard

Jesus does not always pass in our life with a miracle [even though] ... he always makes himself heard. Always. And when the Lord passes [by], what happened here [the miraculous catch of fish by Peter, James, and John] always occurs. He tells us something, he makes us understand something, then he says a word to us which is a promise; he asks something of us in our way of life, he asks us to give up something, to renounce something.

And he then gives us a mission.

— Homily, Domus Sanctae Marthae, September 5, 2013

Reflection: Where is God making himself heard in your life? What is he asking you to give up or renounce? What mission is he calling you on? Re-commit yourself to what he is telling you. Double your efforts to respond to the Lord's call.

Proof That God Is Not With Him

Humility is what gives assurance that the Lord is there. When someone is self-sufficient, when he has all the answers to every question, it is proof that God is not with him.

— *On Heaven and Earth: Pope Francis on Faith, Family, and the Church in the 21st Century*

Reflection: St. Ignatius of Loyola once said, "Pray as though everything depended on God. Work as though everything depended on you." Where is God calling you to trust more in him? Where is he calling you to work harder? Ask for the grace to live out this balance.

Mutated Hearts

Love is the greatest power for the transformation of reality because it pulls down the walls of selfishness and fills the ditches that keep us apart. This is the love that comes from a mutated heart, from a heart of stone that has been turned into a heart of flesh, a human heart.

— Address, June 17, 2013

Reflection: Reflect on your own heart. What parts of it are stony, what parts are mutated? Where do you need healing so that you can better love others?

The Logic of the Gospel

Jesus' disciple renounces all his possessions because in Jesus he has found the greatest Good in which every other good receives its full value and meaning: family ties, other relationships, work, cultural and economic goods and so forth....

The Christian detaches him- or herself from all things and rediscovers all things in the logic of the Gospel, the logic of love and of service.

— Angelus address, September 8, 2013

Reflection: Take a moment to think about your own logic of love and service toward family, work, and your possessions. Do you value Jesus the most? Do you make the logic of the Gospel a priority?

This Is Interesting: God Is Joyful!

CHRISTMAS EVE

God is joyful. This is interesting: God is joyful! And what is the joy of God? The joy of God is forgiving, the joy of God is forgiving! The joy of a shepherd who finds his little lamb; the joy of a woman who finds her coin; it is the joy of a father welcoming home the son who was lost, who was as though dead and has come back to life, who has come home. Here is the entire Gospel! Here! The whole Gospel, all of Christianity, is here!

But make sure that it is not sentiment; it is not being a "do-gooder"! On the contrary, mercy is the true force that can save man and the world from the "cancer" that is sin, moral evil, spiritual evil. Only love fills the void, the negative chasms that evil opens in hearts and in history. Only love can do this, and this is God's joy!

— Angelus address, September 15, 2013

Reflection: God wants to forgive you. He wants you to know his mercy and to give this mercy to others. How can your life better reflect this reality? Do you need to go to confession more frequently? Do you need to more readily forgive others? Ask God what he wants you to do with this great gift of mercy.

God Has a Real Face

CHRISTMAS

After Jesus has come into the world, it is impossible to act as if we do not know God, or as if he were something that is abstract, empty, a purely nominal reference. No, God has a real face, he has a name: God is mercy, God is faithfulness, he is life which is given to us all.

— Angelus address, August 11, 2013

Reflection: What does the gift of Christmas mean to you? How does Jesus' birth make your faith more real and more human? Celebrate the joy of his arrival.

The Blood of the Martyrs

FEAST OF ST. STEPHEN

"If one member suffers, all suffer together; if one member is honored, all rejoice together" (1 Corinthians 12:26). This is a law of the Christian life, and in this sense we can say that there is also an ecumenism of suffering: just as the blood of the martyrs was a seed of strength and fertility for the Church, so too the sharing of daily sufferings can become an effective instrument of unity.

— Address, May 10, 2013

Reflection: The martyrs of the Church show us how to embrace suffering for the faith. Where is God calling you to suffer? How can this suffering help you to be unified with others? Find time to hear someone else's struggles, and make a point to pray for them.

The New Things of God

You see, the new things of God are not like the novelties of this world, all of which are temporary; they come and go, and we keep looking for more. The new things which God gives to our lives are lasting, not only in the future, when we will be with him, but today as well.

God is even now making all things new; the Holy Spirit is truly transforming us, and through us he also wants to transform the world in which we live.

— Homily, Holy Mass With the Rite of Confirmation,
April 28, 2013

Reflection: What temporary things in life do you hold on to? Where is God asking you to move on or let go? How can you release these things in your heart and invite the Holy Spirit to give you something greater and lasting?

The Gospel of Life

FEAST OF THE HOLY INNOCENTS

[There] is the idea that rejecting God, the message of Christ, the Gospel of Life, will somehow lead to freedom, to complete human fulfillment. As a result, the Living God is replaced by fleeting human idols, which offer the intoxication of a flash of freedom but in the end bring new forms of slavery and death.

— Homily, June 16, 2013

Reflection: In your life, where are you tempted to choose death over life? Where do you choose selfishness over the gift of self? Make it a priority to give of yourself in a true and meaningful way to others this week.

Ancient Rule for Pilgrims

There is an ancient rule for pilgrims, which St. Ignatius adopts, and which is why I know it! In one of his rules, he says that the person accompanying the pilgrim must walk at his or her pace, not going on ahead or falling behind. In other words, I envisage a Church that knows how to walk with men and women along the path. The pilgrim's rule will help inspire us.

— Address, September 21, 2013

Reflection: Whom is God calling you to walk beside? Ask the Holy Spirit to help you walk at the same pace, accompanying others where they are, not where you'd like them to be.

Grow and Become Strong

The Gospel of St. Luke tells us that, in the family of Nazareth, Jesus "grew and became strong, filled with wisdom; and the favor of God was upon him" (Luke 2:40). Our Lady does just this for us: she helps us to grow as human beings and in the faith, to be strong and never to fall into the temptation of being human beings and Christians in a superficial way, but to live responsibly, to strive ever higher.

— Address, May 4, 2013

Reflection: It's been said that it takes about a month to form a habit. Consider an area of your life where you need to grow in virtue, and spend the next month developing the corresponding good behavior. Entrust this habit-forming time to Mary.

No Peace Without Truth

Francis of Assisi tells us we should work to build peace. But there is no true peace without truth! There cannot be true peace if everyone is his own criterion, if everyone can always claim exclusively his own rights, without at the same time caring for the good of others, of everyone, on the basis of the nature that unites every human being on this earth.

— Address, March 22, 2013

Reflection: Where can you find the truth that can give you peace? Take time to read the *Catechism of the Catholic Church*. Make it a New Year's resolution to read just one paragraph each day in the coming year. His truth will bring you peace!

Index

About the Editor

Kevin Cotter is a missionary with FOCUS (the Fellowship of Catholic University Students), where he serves as the Director of Curriculum and Web. As the creator of PopeAlarm.com, Kevin notified over one hundred thousand people about Pope Francis' election via text and e-mail. He holds an M.A. in Sacred Scripture from the Augustine Institute and lives in Denver, Colorado, with his wife, Lisa, and their young children. Kevin dedicates his work on this book to Lisa: "Thank you for all of your love and support along this journey of ours."